Reuniting the Nation:
A Blueprint for Unity and Global Identity

Demetri D. Long

Dedication

May we grow old together in a world that reflects the unity and greatness we both dream of—a nation where divisions fade, and hope thrives. For all the love we share and the vision of a brighter future we hold, this book is a small step toward the world I hope we build together. I love you, Nick.

Part I: Understanding Polarization

"If we don't hang together, we shall surely hang separately."
- Benjamin Franklin, 1776

The Divided States of America

The global economic, cultural, technological, and militaristic superpower since the 1990s *was* unquestionably the United States of America.

That name, *the United States of America*, elicits imagery of impactful influence, unstoppable strength, and above all, unshakable unity. The county's name represents a collective of different states with their own distinctive peoples under a common flag. Its founding fathers embraced a "Join or Die" mentality as they recognized that divided states could never wield the influence of a great power. And many of their successors also recognized this fact; after all, it was the 16th President of the United States, Abraham Lincoln, who famously declared, "A house divided against itself cannot stand."

And yet, as I sit at my cluttered desk—provided by my college and bearing the marks of countless students before me, with its scuffed edges, engraved initials, and stubbornly sticky drawers—I can't escape the nagging realization that those four words carry a weight they no longer bear. That is to say—in truth—the United States of America has become a misnomer. It's a title from another, more distant era. An era that no longer reflects the fractured reality of our current century. Today, as unfortunate as that might be, we are the *divided* nations of America, severed between political, economic, and cultural lines. In other words, we are a nation divided yet forced to stand.

Perhaps you've felt it too. The unease in a conversation with a friend or family member when politics comes up. The hesitation to share your opinion online, knowing one wrong post could cost you your career, rescind your college acceptance, or even spark the end of a relationship. Even holidays are no longer safe havens for love and gratitude but have become battlegrounds, where people retreat to their ideological corners or clash with rehearsed, endlessly repeated talking points. The divisions are undeniable. And they are tearing us apart.

Put simply, the U.S. was not always like this. There were times when our differences strengthened us. Debate is the cornerstone of democracy. Think of the unity after Pearl Harbor or how the U.S. put a man on the moon (an achievement that has yet to be matched). Today, however, we are playing a zero-sum game where one side's victory *requires* the other side's complete annihilation. We know not of compromise.

Take, for example, the 2018-2019 U.S. government shutdown, lasting 35 days and 35 nights, which was the longest in American history. This shutdown resulted in a little under a million federal workers going unpaid, interrupted public services like the TSA, and inflicted a permanent cost of $3 billion on the U.S. economy.

"How did this happen?" I hear a curious reader ask.

Well, both sides—the Democrats and Republicans—viewed the issue of funding for a border wall as a zero-sum game. The Republican-dominated Trump administration believed that the border wall was non-negotiable. It was a necessity for national security and the proper step in protecting Americans from illegal immigration, causing the Republicans to refuse to sign any funding bill without proper allocation to building the border wall. Meanwhile, Democrats believed that the border wall was a symbol of a divisive, ineffective immigration policy. In their eyes, even under pressure, there was no alternative: there would be no funding for a bill that supported the border wall.

Ultimately, neither side achieved a definitive win. The shutdown ended with no immediate wall funding (only additional funding for border security) and unresolved long-term tension around immigration policy that would become even more contentious in the 2020 and 2024 elections. In addition to the nation's loss of $3 billion, there was an annihilation of public trust and stability. In the end, the entire nation bore the brunt of the stalemate, illustrating the destructive and costly nature of polarization.

These moments are not isolated incidents. They are symptomatic of a larger, ongoing fracture in our nation's foundation—a division rooted in decades of political, cultural, and economic shifts. What was once a nation united by shared struggles and common purpose has devolved into partisan gridlock, cultural wars, and economic disparity.

So how did we get here? How did the "United" States become so divided? To answer these questions, we must examine the *roots of division* that have shaped our modern reality.

The Roots of Division

To understand our present, we must examine our past. Polarization is not a new phenomenon in American history; it is woven into the very fabric of our national identity. From the fierce debates between Federalists and Anti-Federalists over the balance of power in the fledgling republic to the bloody Civil War that tore the nation apart over slavery, division has always played a central role in shaping the United States. These moments of strife were not simply disagreements—they were battles over the soul of the nation, over what it means to be "American."

However, the nature and intensity of these divides have evolved over time. In the early years of the republic, ideological conflicts were often tempered by a shared commitment to building a unified nation. Even during moments of profound crisis, such as the Civil War, there was an understanding of the need to reconcile

3

and rebuild. For instance, at the war's end, the surrender at Appomattox Courthouse demonstrated a deliberate effort to foster reconciliation, with Union General Ulysses S. Grant offering generous terms to Confederate soldiers, allowing them to return home with their horses and mules to aid in rebuilding their lives. Similarly, the Freedmen's Bureau, established during Reconstruction, sought to address the inequalities left by slavery while providing food, education, and legal assistance to formerly enslaved people and poor white Southerners. These efforts, though imperfect, reflected a recognition that unity required practical support and shared efforts to rebuild the nation.

Today, however, the divides we face are more fragmented and pervasive, extending beyond politics into our culture, economy, and even daily interactions. Where debates once sought resolution and reintegration, modern polarization often prioritizes domination, making it increasingly difficult to achieve the spirit of reconciliation that once allowed the nation to heal.

In the past, divisions were often anchored in clear, tangible issues—slavery, suffrage, civil rights. These deeply contentious battles were fought over concrete policies, laws, and rights. While painful and divisive, they often had defined goals and resolutions. Today, our divisions are more diffuse, seeping into every aspect of our lives. They shape the news we consume, the neighborhoods we live in, the brands we buy, and even the identities we embrace. This shift from focused political disputes to pervasive cultural and societal rifts makes our divides not only harder to address but also more deeply entrenched.

So, when we ask why polarization feels so entrenched, it's easy to fall into the trap of thinking it's because humans are just morally flawed, hopelessly divided by their inability to get along. I too was convinced that it had to be some fundamental failing of humanity—maybe selfishness, maybe tribalism. Yet, the answer isn't some grand conspiracy or moral failing. It's far simpler than that it's structural, stupid!

Four primary factors fuel polarization: political structures, media

4

and technology, economic disparities, and cultural and social differences. These elements don't operate in isolation; they reinforce one another, creating a web of division that feels increasingly difficult to untangle. But let's start with the political, because if we're honest, much of the chaos stems from how the system itself is designed.

At its core, the problem isn't just about bad actors or partisan bickering—it's the rules of the game. Gerrymandering is the practice of manipulating the boundaries of electoral districts to give one political party an unfair advantage. By carefully drawing district lines, politicians can "pack" voters who support the opposition into a few districts or "crack" them across multiple districts, diluting their influence. This process often results in oddly shaped districts that prioritize political gain over fair representation. Gerrymandering undermines democracy by allowing politicians to choose their voters instead of voters choosing their representatives.

This structure doesn't just allow polarization; it actively incentivizes it. The Princeton Gerrymandering Project, for instance, highlights how gerrymandered congressional districts exacerbate polarization through mathematical truths. By creating a "partisan advantage" for one party, these districts incentivize politicians to appeal to their base rather than seek bipartisan solutions. This dynamic fosters a Congress where compromise becomes rare, and polarization deepens, creating a legislative environment where gridlock is increasingly the norm.

The broader impact of polarization on Congress is striking. According to Quorum, bipartisanship in Congress has declined by 30% (1989-2017), reflecting a steady erosion of cross-party collaboration. A *Vox* analysis visually illustrates this trend, showing how voting patterns have grown more divided along party lines over the decades. While some collaboration remains—Quorum data from the 115th Congress (2017-2019) shows that nearly 70% of laws had bipartisan cosponsorship—the overall decline in bipartisan cooperation highlights a deeper systemic issue. This is because the statistic that 70% of laws in the 115th Congress had bipartisan cosponsorship may sound promising, but it masks a key issue: most of these bills address low-stakes or noncontroversial matters, such as naming post offices or passing ceremonial resolutions. When it comes to major legislation— issues like healthcare reform, immigration policy, or climate change—partisan gridlock dominates.

An example of this dynamic can be observed in the 115th Congress (2017–2019). While a significant portion of enacted legislation had bipartisan cosponsorship, many of these were low-stakes measures. For instance, numerous bills were passed to name post offices, such as H.R. 1496, which designated a facility in Los Angeles as the "Marvin Gaye Post Office." A bill that had 72 cosponsors. These types of bills, while honoring individuals and communities, do not tackle contentious or systemic issues.

In contrast, attempts to pass significant legislation, such as the repeal of the Affordable Care Act (ACA), highlighted deep partisan divides. Efforts to dismantle the ACA passed in the House of Representatives and ultimately failed in the Senate due to a lack of sufficient support. This bill, might I add, had 0 cosponsors. Similarly, major immigration reforms and climate change initiatives have repeatedly stalled because of partisan gridlock, underscoring the difficulty of achieving bipartisan consensus on transformative issues.

Overall, gerrymandering exacerbates these trends by discouraging moderation. Politicians in "safe seats" have little incentive to reach across the aisle, as their primary threat often comes from within their own party rather than from general election opponents. This structural flaw amplifies polarization, turning Congress into a battleground where collaboration is the exception rather than the rule. By prioritizing partisan advantage over fair representation, gerrymandering deepens polarization, entrenching ideological divides and making collaboration within the legislative process increasingly rare.

Another key driver of polarization is the rise of media and technology. In the mid-20th century, Americans largely consumed news from a handful of trusted sources. Television networks like CBS, NBC, and ABC offered a shared narrative, even if viewers disagreed on how to interpret it. Walter Cronkite, often called "the most trusted man in America," ended his broadcasts with a simple yet unifying phrase: "And that's the way it is."

Today, the idea of a shared narrative feels almost quaint. The rise of cable news in the 1990s, followed by the explosion of digital and social media, has created a fractured and polarized information ecosystem. Cable networks like Fox News and MSNBC cater to opposite ends of the political spectrum, curating narratives tailored to their audience's beliefs rather than presenting balanced perspectives. This bifurcation set the stage for an even more chaotic and divisive era: the age of digital media.

Platforms like Facebook and Twitter amplify content that fuels outrage and division, driven by algorithms designed to maximize engagement. Research consistently shows that posts evoking anger or fear are far more likely to be shared, creating echo chambers that reinforce existing worldviews and entrench ideological divides (one of which is this peer-reviewed article). But even as these platforms dominate discussions about misinformation and polarization, another major player has quietly risen to prominence: YouTube.

YouTube has become a dominant source of information for millions of people worldwide. According to the Pew Research Center, nearly a quarter of U.S. adults get their news from YouTube, where a vast and often unregulated network of content creators has flourished. Unlike traditional media outlets, many YouTubers have no formal training in journalism and are not held accountable to editorial standards. Instead, they often operate independently, blending opinion, entertainment, and selective facts to engage audiences.

The platform's financial incentives exacerbate the issue. Successful YouTubers can earn substantial income through ad revenue, sponsorships, and direct donations from viewers, often via platforms like Patreon. These revenue streams create a powerful incentive to cater to niche or extreme audiences, where sensationalism, conspiratorial thinking, or hyper-partisan rhetoric are rewarded with loyalty and financial support. In this landscape, credibility takes a back seat to charisma, as creators vie for attention and clicks rather than striving for factual accuracy.

Traditional media outlets, faced with declining viewership and shrinking revenues, have also adapted to this hyper-polarized environment. To remain relevant in a world dominated by digital platforms, even established news organizations often adopt the same tactics of sensationalism and targeted content. Headlines are crafted to maximize clicks, commentary increasingly replaces objective reporting, and many outlets lean into partisan branding to secure a loyal audience base. This shift blurs the lines between journalism and entertainment, further eroding public trust and contributing to polarization.

The convergence of these trends creates a troubling information ecosystem. As traditional gatekeepers lose their central role, audiences fragment into smaller, ideologically homogeneous groups. YouTube and other digital platforms amplify this fragmentation by rewarding creators who prioritize engagement over accuracy. Meanwhile, traditional outlets, striving to compete, adopt similar tactics, leaving little room for balanced, nuanced reporting.

This fractured landscape means there is no shared foundation of facts or common ground for debate. Instead, opposing "realities" compete for dominance, making meaningful dialogue between differing perspectives nearly impossible. The rise of YouTube and the transformation of traditional media illustrate a paradox: while the democratization of information has empowered more voices, it has also enabled the proliferation of misinformation and hyper-partisanship. In this environment, the idea of a shared narrative isn't just quaint—it feels like something left behind in a time long past.

Most Americans recognize the significant role misinformation and media bias play in exacerbating political divides. According to a 2022 study by the Knight Foundation, 61% of Americans feel that it has become increasingly difficult to stay well-informed. This widespread sentiment reflects a collective frustration with a fragmented and sensationalized media landscape that often obscures the full picture, leaving citizens grappling with incomplete or skewed information.

This awareness stems from lived experiences in a polarized media environment. People see how cable news outlets tailor narratives to their audiences, how social media algorithms amplify outrage, and how YouTube creators profit from sensational content with little accountability. They recognize that these dynamics don't just inform political opinions—they entrench ideological divides, making compromise and mutual understanding increasingly elusive.

Despite this shared understanding, addressing the problem remains a challenge. While most Americans can agree on the harm caused by misinformation and bias, solutions are harder to come by. The same study revealed that trust in media institutions is "the lowest level Gallup and Knight have recorded in the past five years.". This mistrust, combined with the rapid evolution of digital platforms, perpetuates a cycle where polarization thrives despite the widespread acknowledgment of its causes.

But media is not the only culprit. Economic inequality has also played a significant role in driving division. For decades, the American Dream promised upward mobility—a belief that hard work and determination would lead to success, regardless of where you started. But for many, that promise feels broken. Wages have stagnated, the cost of living has soared, and wealth has become increasingly concentrated at the top. These economic realities fuel resentment and despair, creating fertile ground for division.

The economic disparities between towns like Palo Alto, California, and Hazard, Kentucky, are often framed as cultural differences, but at their core, they are fundamentally economic challenges. The stark contrast between Palo Alto's median household income of $214,118 in 2022, driven by the thriving tech industry, and Hazard's $65,846, where the coal industry has been in steady decline, creates divergent priorities for residents.

However, these differing priorities—such as Palo Alto's focus on climate change and tech innovation versus Hazard's emphasis on job creation and economic survival—are rooted in the economic realities of their respective communities.

Politicians and media narratives frequently transform these economic challenges into cultural battles, pitting communities against each other. Climate change, for example, becomes a flashpoint not because residents in Hazard deny its existence, but because proposed solutions often fail to address their immediate economic needs, like job security and industry revitalization. Similarly, Palo Alto's push for green innovation isn't about dismissing working-class struggles but stems from the economic opportunities its residents see in the tech-driven green economy.

The problem lies in how these issues are framed. By casting them as cultural divides, the underlying economic inequities are obscured, making it seem as though the two communities are ideologically opposed when they are really seeking solutions to the same fundamental problem: economic stability. With the right policies—such as investments in renewable energy jobs in Appalachia or federal support for transitioning industries—these supposed cultural differences could dissolve. Residents of Hazard and Palo Alto alike want secure jobs, thriving communities, and a sustainable future, but they've been forced into opposition by narratives that prioritize division over shared economic progress.

This economic framing, warped into cultural conflict, underscores how deeply intertwined our divisions have become. What starts as a matter of livelihood quickly evolves into questions of identity and values, further amplified by political rhetoric and media narratives. It's a pattern that extends beyond just economic issues, feeding into the broader landscape of cultural and social differences—arguably the last major piece of the polarization puzzle. These cultural divides, often shaped by race, religion, education, and regional identity, reinforce and deepen the fractures in our society, making them harder to bridge. Let's explore how these cultural and social differences entrench polarization and why they continue to resist efforts at reconciliation.

Statistics paint a grim picture of the personal toll these divides exact, particularly as they intersect with cultural and social differences. According to a 2022 Gallup poll, the "majority of U.S. adults (57%) say they have at times avoided sharing their political views because of fear of harassment or poor treatment". Meanwhile, a 2021 survey by the American Survey Center found that 15% of Americans have ended a friendship over political disagreements, with Democrats twice as likely as Republicans to do so (20% vs. 10%). These numbers aren't just statistics—they reflect a society pulling apart, where even personal relationships can't withstand the weight of cultural and ideological differences.

Take the response to the COVID-19 pandemic as an example. What might have been a unifying national effort—akin to the collective resolve seen after Pearl Harbor or 9/11—became a cultural flashpoint. Mask mandates, vaccination campaigns, and lockdowns were no longer just public health measures but deeply polarizing symbols. A 2021 Kaiser Family Foundation survey found that 87% of Democrats believed "the fact that most vaccinated people who become infected with COVID-19 do not require hospitalization means that the vaccines are working", compared to just 55% of Republicans. Additionally, the same study found that 39% of Republicans believed "the fact that some vaccinated people are becoming infected with COVID-19 means that the vaccines are not working," while only 10% of Democrats believed that. These differences went beyond policy preferences—they reflected competing worldviews about individual freedom, collective responsibility, and trust in institutions. Instead of rallying together, Americans splintered, with states pursuing drastically different policies and citizens viewing one another with growing suspicion.

Our residential choices increasingly mirror and reinforce our political divisions. A 2020 analysis by the *Daily Yonder* revealed that in the 1976 presidential election, about 26% of Americans lived in "landslide counties," where one candidate won by a significant margin. By 2020, this figure had risen to nearly

58.2%, indicating a substantial increase in politically homogeneous communities. This geographic polarization fosters environments where prevailing political beliefs go unchallenged, leading to echo chambers that intensify partisan perspectives. The implications of this geographic sorting are profound. When communities become politically uniform, residents are less likely to engage with differing perspectives, making compromise and understanding more difficult. As Americans increasingly live, work, and socialize among those who share their political leanings, the bonds that once bridged cultural and social differences continue to weaken, leaving the nation more divided than ever.

Perhaps most alarming is the erosion of trust in democracy itself, a crisis that reflects deep cultural fractures. A 2022 survey by the Institute for Democracy and Electoral Assistance found that 64% of Americans believe the nation's democratic system is at risk of failure. This lack of trust cuts across party lines. Republicans frequently cite concerns about election integrity, while Democrats worry about voter suppression. Both narratives stem from cultural anxieties, shaped and reinforced by partisan leaders and media echo chambers.

In such a polarized landscape, the blame game flourishes. Rural communities blame urban elites for ignoring their struggles. Working-class whites blame immigrants for economic hardships. Millennials blame baby boomers for environmental and economic challenges. These narratives of blame are perpetuated by political leaders who exploit cultural tensions as a tool for mobilizing their bases. Rather than addressing systemic issues, they frame conflicts as battles between irreconcilable identities, deepening divisions.

The roots of division are undeniably deep, and cultural differences make them even harder to navigate. However, history offers lessons: America has faced profound polarization before and found ways to mend it. Whether we can rise to this challenge again will determine not only the future of democracy but also the meaning of the American identity itself. If left unaddressed, these divides threaten to fracture the very fabric of what it means to be a united nation—of what it means to be American.

The Personal Toll of Polarization

Political polarization—the deepening ideological divide between opposing viewpoints—has become a defining feature of contemporary society. To address it effectively, one must first understand its roots, which lie not only in external influences like media and political systems but also in the biological and psychological factors that shape individual political orientations. These internal mechanisms influence how people process information, form group identities, and respond to conflict. Recognizing these factors is essential to developing strategies that can bridge divides and foster greater understanding across ideological lines.

Research indicates that certain brain structures are associated with political leanings. A 2011 study by Ryota Kanai and colleagues at University College London found that individuals with conservative views tend to have a larger amygdala, a region involved in processing emotions like fear and threat detection. Conversely, those with liberal views exhibited increased gray matter volume in the anterior cingulate cortex, which plays a role in managing uncertainty and conflicting information. These findings suggest that inherent neurological differences may influence how individuals perceive and react to political information.

Further supporting this, a 2024 replication study involving 928 participants confirmed the association between amygdala size and conservative tendencies, though with a smaller effect size than the original study. This underscores the complex interplay between brain structure and political ideology, indicating that while biological factors contribute, they are not the sole determinants of political orientation.

Psychological factors also significantly contribute to political polarization. Individuals often process information in ways that reinforce their preexisting beliefs, a phenomenon known as confirmation bias. This bias leads people to favor information that aligns with their views and dismiss opposing perspectives, deepening ideological divides.

Emotional responses also play a crucial role. Partisan individuals exhibit distinct neural responses to political messages, especially those emphasizing threat, morality, and emotion. These responses can intensify partisan identities and reduce openness to alternative viewpoints.

Social identity theory further explains polarization by suggesting that individuals derive a sense of belonging from group affiliations, including political parties. This affiliation fosters in-group favoritism and out-group hostility, leading to an "us versus them" mentality that hinders constructive dialogue and compromise.

The interaction between biological predispositions and psychological processes creates a feedback loop that exacerbates polarization. For instance, individuals with a heightened sensitivity to threats may gravitate toward conservative ideologies that emphasize security and stability. This alignment reinforces their threat sensitivity, making them more receptive to messages that highlight danger or moral transgressions.

Conversely, those with a greater tolerance for uncertainty may be drawn to liberal ideologies that prioritize change and diversity. Their cognitive flexibility allows them to process complex, conflicting information, making them more open to progressive policies.

Understanding these dynamics is crucial for addressing polarization. Recognizing that biological and psychological factors shape political beliefs can foster empathy and reduce the tendency to view opposing partisans as irrational or malicious. This awareness can promote more constructive engagement across ideological divides.

Additionally, creating environments that reduce perceived threats—both physical and cultural—can lower defensive reactions and open individuals to compromise. Policies that address economic and social insecurities may alleviate the fear and uncertainty that drive individuals toward polarized positions.

In conclusion, political polarization is a multifaceted phenomenon rooted in both biological predispositions and psychological processes. By acknowledging and addressing these underlying factors, society can work toward bridging divides and fostering a more cohesive and understanding political environment.

Why This Book?

Books have the power to transform perspectives and foster meaningful conversations. Unlike the fleeting debates of social media or the soundbites dominating cable news, books encourage readers to pause, reflect, and engage with complex ideas. They provide the depth and nuance necessary to address intricate problems, tell stories that connect on a human level, and propose solutions that are thoughtful and substantive.

This book aims to do more than just diagnose the fractures in our society—it strives to reimagine what we could be. What would a more united America look like? How can we create a society where differences are valued rather than feared, where debates build bridges instead of walls, and where progress is defined not by winning but by how much we achieve together?

You should read this book because it's not just another commentary on what's broken—it's a roadmap for how to fix it. Grounded in research, real-world examples, and actionable strategies, this book doesn't aim to preach or polarize but to inform and inspire. It acknowledges the complexity of our divisions while offering hope through practical solutions. Whether you're frustrated by the state of our society, eager to bridge divides in your own community, or simply searching for a deeper understanding of how we got here, this book will guide you with clarity and purpose.

What makes this book trustworthy is its commitment to balance and evidence. It draws from a wide range of perspectives—academic studies, historical examples, and personal stories—to provide a nuanced view of polarization and its solutions. It avoids sensationalism, focusing instead on what's

15

achievable through collaboration and shared goals. This isn't a book that promises easy answers or quick fixes; it's a thoughtful, honest exploration of what it will take to rebuild trust and unity. If you're ready to move past blame and toward understanding, this book is a place to start.

Why Now?

The urgency of this book cannot be overstated. The longer we allow polarization to fester, the harder it will be to reverse. Every day that passes without addressing this issue is another day of missed opportunities, strained relationships, and unaddressed challenges. But there's also reason for hope. The fact that so many Americans recognize the problem suggests that we're ready for change.

This book is not just about ideas; it's about action. As you read, I hope you'll see yourself not as a passive observer, but as an active participant in the work of depolarization. Whether it's starting a conversation with someone who sees the world differently, getting involved in local initiatives, or simply reflecting on your own biases, every step matters.

The house may be divided, but it hasn't fallen. And it doesn't have to. Together, we can repair the cracks, reinforce the foundation, and ensure that this house—a house big enough for all of us—stands strong for generations to come. This book is an invitation to begin that work, and I'm honored to take this journey with you.

I am writing this book not just because I see the dangers of polarization but because I believe in the possibility of unity. I believe that beneath our differences lies a shared humanity—a common desire for safety, opportunity, and dignity. I believe that America's strength has always come from its diversity, not just of race and culture but of ideas, perspectives, and experiences.

This book is not about assigning blame. It's not about proving one side right and the other wrong. It's about understanding why we're so divided and exploring how we can begin to bridge those divides. It's about challenging ourselves to see the world through the eyes of others, to question our own assumptions, and to seek common ground even when it feels elusive.

In the chapters that follow, we'll delve deeper into the forces driving polarization, from political systems to media algorithms, economic inequality, and cultural identity. We'll explore strategies for depolarization, from building empathy and reforming education to holding leaders accountable and promoting a global identity. And in the final chapter, we'll imagine a future where America is truly united—not through uniformity but through a shared commitment to equity, justice, and collaboration.

This journey won't be easy. Depolarization requires us to step out of our comfort zones, to engage with people and ideas that challenge us, and to confront the systems that perpetuate division. But I believe it's worth it. Because the alternative—a nation perpetually at war with itself—is simply unsustainable.

As you read this book, I invite you to approach it with an open mind and a willing heart. Together, we can begin to chart a path forward. Together, we can rediscover the promise of a united America.

And together, we can prove that *the United States of America* is not just a name—it's a reality worth fighting for.

The History of Division

Polarization didn't emerge overnight. It's a culmination of choices, events, and systems that have compounded over centuries. To understand the stark divides of today, we must first trace the roots of our divisions—because history doesn't just inform our present; it shapes it. The echo of past conflicts, compromises, and cultural clashes reverberates through every modern political debate. Understanding polarization isn't possible without understanding how we got here.

Imagine sitting in the audience at a heated 1858 debate between Abraham Lincoln and Stephen Douglas. The air is tense, the crowd divided. The issue: whether slavery should expand into new territories. Both men represent polarized views, but at their core, the debate reflects a deeper fracture—a nation grappling with what it means to be free, equal, and united. Sound familiar? That same tension—the fight over identity, power, and belonging—continues to play out in different forms today.

America's history is a story of contradictions: freedom and oppression, unity and division, progress and backlash. The Revolutionary War united disparate colonies but left unresolved questions about slavery, indigenous rights, and class inequalities. The Civil War was fought to preserve the Union, but Reconstruction saw that unity unravel under the weight of systemic racism. The Civil Rights Movement sought justice, but its victories ignited new cultural battlegrounds. Each era pushed the pendulum of division and unity back and forth, setting the stage for the polarized landscape we inhabit now.

History offers invaluable lessons. It teaches us that division isn't just about disagreements over policy—it's about competing narratives of who we are as a nation and who we want to be. It shows us how unchecked divisions fester and erupt into conflict, and it reminds us that unity requires hard, uncomfortable work. By exploring the patterns of our past, we can better understand the roots of today's polarization—and how to overcome it.

So, let's dig in. To understand why we're so divided today, we must first uncover the fault lines of history that brought us here. Only then can we begin to bridge them.

Founding Era (1776–1820)

The United States was born out of ideological tension. The Founding Fathers, though united in their fight for independence, were deeply divided over the nature and scope of federal power. These debates, driven by competing visions of governance, laid the groundwork for the nation's first political fault lines and would influence divisions that persist to this day.

Alexander Hamilton and Patrick Henry represent two sharply opposing visions that shaped the foundational debate over the U.S. Constitution. Their contrasting views highlight a core tension that has persisted throughout American history: the balance between centralized authority and individual or state autonomy. By examining their arguments, we can trace the roots of America's political polarization and the enduring debate over the role of government.

Hamilton, a staunch Federalist, viewed a strong central government as essential for national survival and progress. In Federalist No. 1, he famously framed the stakes of the Constitutional debate:

It has been frequently remarked that it seems to have been

19

reserved to the people of this country, by their conduct and example, to decide the important question, whether societies of men are really capable or not of establishing good government from reflection and choice, or whether they are forever destined to depend for their political constitutions on accident and force. If there be any truth in the remark, the crisis at which we are arrived may with propriety be regarded as the era in which that decision is to be made; and a wrong election of the part we shall act may, in this view, deserve to be considered as the general misfortune of mankind.

Hamilton argued that the Constitution was not just a practical framework but a test of humanity's ability to govern itself through reason and deliberation. To him, the Articles of Confederation had demonstrated the dangers of a weak central government: disunity among states, economic instability, and an inability to defend the nation or enforce treaties. For Hamilton, the Constitution's promise of a unified federal government was a safeguard against chaos, providing the structure necessary for stability, commerce, and international credibility.

Patrick Henry, an Anti-Federalist, saw the Constitution as a betrayal of the Revolution's ideals and a dangerous step toward tyranny. Speaking at the Virginia Ratifying Convention in 1788, he declared:

And here I would make this inquiry of those worthy characters who composed a part of the late federal Convention. I am sure they were fully impressed with the necessity of forming a great consolidated government instead of a confederation. That this is a consolidated government is demonstrably clear; and the danger of such a government is, to my mind, very striking. This is a consolidated government. The question turns, sir, on that poor little thing — the expression, We, the people, instead of the States of America. I need not take much pains to show that the principles of this system are extremely pernicious, impolitic, and dangerous.

Henry's opposition was rooted in a profound distrust of

centralized authority. To him, the phrase "We, the People" symbolized a dangerous shift of power away from the states and toward an overarching federal government that could erode local autonomy. He feared that the proposed system would pave the way for despotism, with distant federal institutions wielding unchecked power over the individual liberties and rights of the states.

Their conflict reflects a deeper philosophical divide. Hamilton's optimism rested on his belief in rational governance and the ability of a central authority to balance competing interests. Henry, however, prioritized safeguarding liberties over the efficiency or power of government, arguing that decentralization was the only way to prevent tyranny. This clash between consolidation and autonomy is not just a historical debate but a recurring theme in American politics.

The significance of this foundational conflict cannot be overstated. Hamilton and Henry's opposing views resonate in contemporary debates about federal versus state power, individual freedoms, and the role of government in addressing national challenges. Whether it's the distribution of resources, healthcare, or environmental policy, these debates echo the same concerns that animated the Federalist and Anti-Federalist divide.

Including their opposition in this book underscores how deeply rooted polarization is in America's founding. The Constitution itself was born out of a compromise between these conflicting visions, with the Bill of Rights added to placate Anti-Federalist concerns about protecting individual liberties. By understanding these historical debates, we gain insight into the enduring tensions that shape American political life and the delicate balance required to maintain unity in a nation defined by diversity.

Down the line, these ideological disagreements were formalized in the creation of the nation's first political parties: the Federalist Party and the Democratic-Republican Party. Although their immediate conflicts were political, they exposed deeper cultural and economic divides. The Federalists represented urban, industrializing regions in the North, while the Anti-Federalists found their base in the agrarian South and frontier regions. These tensions not only defined early American politics but also sowed the seeds for sectionalism and regional conflict.

The ideological divisions between Federalists and Anti-Federalists deepened as the nation expanded, particularly by 1820. Economic disparities played a central role, with the North embracing burgeoning industrialization and commerce, while the South remained entrenched in agriculture and the institution of slavery. These diverging paths shaped not only the economies of these regions but also their cultural and political identities. The Missouri Compromise of 1820 exemplified the nation's struggle to balance these opposing forces, temporarily easing tensions between free and slave states but also exposing the fault lines that would widen in the decades to come. These cracks in the nation's foundation laid the groundwork for the Antebellum and Civil War Era (1820–1865), a period marked by intensifying regional divides and the eventual confrontation of America's greatest moral and constitutional crisis.

Antebellum and Civil War Era (1820–1865)

The Missouri Compromise was an early attempt to address sectional tensions, but it ultimately underscored the deepening divide. Missouri's application for statehood in 1819 threatened to upset the balance of power between free and slave states in Congress. After fierce debate, Congress enacted a compromise in 1820 that admitted Missouri as a slave state and Maine as a free state, maintaining the balance. Additionally, it prohibited slavery in the Louisiana Territory north of the 36°30′ latitude line.

The Missouri Compromise temporarily alleviated tensions between the North and South, but it also underscored the growing sectional divide. For the North, restricting the expansion of slavery was seen as a moral necessity and a step toward limiting the institution's reach. In contrast, the South viewed such restrictions as a direct threat to their economic and cultural survival, deepening their resolve to defend slavery. Rather than resolving the underlying conflict, the compromise served as a fragile truce, with both sides becoming increasingly entrenched in their positions (sounds familiar?). As new territories sought admission to the Union, the contentious question of whether they would allow slavery resurfaced time and again, reigniting the very tensions the compromise had sought to ease.

Then, building on the temporary balance achieved by the Missouri Compromise, the question of slavery's expansion continued to fester as the nation grew westward. By the 1850s, the fragile equilibrium was again challenged, leading to new and more contentious legislation. The Kansas-Nebraska Act, spearheaded by Illinois Senator Stephen A. Douglas, sought to address the issue through the principle of popular sovereignty. This legislation allowed settlers in the Kansas and Nebraska territories to decide for themselves whether to permit slavery, effectively nullifying the Missouri Compromise's prohibition of slavery north of the 36°30′ line.

Douglas's intent was to facilitate westward expansion and promote the construction of a transcontinental railroad. However, the act reignited national tensions over slavery, leading to violent conflicts in Kansas between pro-slavery and anti-slavery settlers—a period known as "Bleeding Kansas." The Kansas-Nebraska Act's reliance on popular sovereignty failed to provide a peaceful solution to the slavery debate, instead exacerbating sectional divisions and propelling the nation closer to civil war.

The Kansas-Nebraska Act of 1854 had profound political repercussions, notably contributing to the dissolution of the Whig Party and the emergence of the Republican Party. The Whig Party, already weakened by internal divisions, found itself unable to reconcile its Northern and Southern factions in the face of the Act's implications. The Northern Whigs' opposition to the expansion of slavery clashed irreconcilably with the Southern Whigs' support for the Act, leading to the party's fragmentation and eventual collapse.

In the wake of the Whig Party's disintegration, a new political entity emerged. The Republican Party was formed by a coalition of anti-slavery Northern Whigs, disaffected Democrats, Free-Soilers, and abolitionists, all unified in their opposition to the extension of slavery into the western territories. This realignment transformed the political landscape, turning slavery from a regional concern into a central national issue and further polarizing the country along sectional lines.

The Supreme Court's 1857 decision in *Dred Scott v. Sandford* marked a critical turning point in the nation's growing sectional divide, further inflaming tensions between the North and South. At a time when legislative compromises like the Missouri Compromise and the Kansas-Nebraska Act had already strained the Union, the ruling dealt a severe blow to hopes that the judiciary might offer a path toward reconciliation. The case arose when Dred Scott, an enslaved man, sued for his freedom after being taken into free territory by his owner, sparking a legal battle that would profoundly shape the nation's trajectory.

Chief Justice Roger B. Taney, in delivering the majority opinion for *Dred Scott v. Sandford*, stated:

> They [African Americans] had for more than a century before been regarded as beings of an inferior order, and altogether unfit to associate with the white race, either in social or political relations; and so far inferior, that they had no rights which the white man was bound to respect.

This ruling not only declared that African Americans, whether free or enslaved, were not citizens of the United States but also reinforced the notion that they had no legal standing or protections under federal law. Furthermore, the Court ruled that Congress had no authority to prohibit slavery in the federal territories, effectively *completely* nullifying the Missouri Compromise of 1820 for all states.

The Dred Scott decision provoked widespread outrage in the Northern states, where many viewed it as a blatant attempt to expand the institution of slavery into free territories. Abraham Lincoln, then an emerging political figure, vehemently opposed the ruling. In a speech addressing the decision, Lincoln argued that it contradicted the fundamental principles of equality outlined in the Declaration of Independence and posed a direct threat to the liberties of all Americans. Whereas conversely, the Southern states welcomed the decision as a validation of their belief that slavery was constitutionally protected. The ruling emboldened pro-slavery advocates, reinforcing their stance against any federal interference with the institution of slavery.

By stripping Congress of the power to regulate slavery in the territories and denying African Americans any legal rights, the Dred Scott decision eliminated potential avenues for compromise. This judicial pronouncement deepened the nation's divisions, making the prospect of a peaceful resolution increasingly unlikely and setting the stage for the eventual secession of Southern states and the onset of the Civil War.

Reconstruction and Gilded Age (1865–1900)

After the Civil War, the Reconstruction Era (1865–1877) represented a bold attempt to address the racial and regional divides that had fractured the United States. Central to this effort were the Reconstruction Amendments—the 13th, 14th, and 15th Amendments—which sought to dismantle the institution of slavery and establish equal rights for African Americans. The 13th Amendment abolished slavery, the 14th Amendment granted citizenship and equal protection under the law, and the 15th Amendment extended voting rights to African American men. These amendments marked significant legal progress, but their enforcement was often weak and uneven, particularly in the South, where resistance to Reconstruction policies was fierce.

The Southern states, devastated by the war and resentful of federal intervention, pushed back against Reconstruction efforts. White supremacist groups like the Ku Klux Klan (KKK) emerged almost immediately after the war, aiming to undermine the progress made by African Americans and to restore white dominance through violence and intimidation. The KKK's actions—from lynchings to the burning of Black schools and churches—highlighted the deep cultural and racial divides that persisted despite the legal abolition of slavery.

Jim Crow laws further institutionalized racial segregation and disenfranchisement in the South. These laws, which emerged in the late 19th century, mandated segregation in public spaces and systematically denied African Americans access to voting through poll taxes, literacy tests, and other discriminatory practices. Despite the protections offered by the Reconstruction Amendments, African Americans were effectively excluded from political and economic life in much of the South, entrenching racial polarization for decades to come.

The federal government's commitment to Reconstruction waned as the 1870s progressed, culminating in the Compromise of 1877. In a contested presidential election, Republican Rutherford B. Hayes was awarded the presidency in exchange for the withdrawal of federal troops from the South. This marked the end of Reconstruction and allowed Southern states to implement discriminatory policies with little fear of federal intervention. The compromise symbolized the abandonment of African Americans' rights and the prioritization of national unity over justice.

While the Reconstruction Era grappled with racial and regional divides, the Gilded Age (1870s–1900) exposed new divisions rooted in economic inequality. Rapid industrialization created unprecedented wealth for a small elite, while many workers endured harsh conditions and low wages. Labor strikes, such as the Pullman Strike of 1894, underscored the growing class tensions as workers protested unfair labor practices and economic exploitation.

Political corruption compounded these issues, with Gilded Age politics characterized by patronage, corporate influence, and a lack of accountability that eroded public trust in government. Efforts to address economic and labor inequalities often fell short, blocked by the immense power of industrialists who shaped policy to serve their interests. These failures set the stage for the Progressive Era, as a new wave of reformers sought to tackle the excesses of capitalism, reduce corruption, and address class inequities. As the nation moved into the 20th century, polarization shifted away from regional divides and began to focus more acutely on class struggles and ideological battles over the role of government in regulating the economy and society.

Progressive and New Deal Eras (1900–1945)

The Progressive Era arose in response to the stark inequalities of the Gilded Age. Reformers sought to curb the power of monopolies, improve labor conditions, and expand political rights. Key legislative efforts included the Sherman Antitrust Act (1890) and the Clayton Antitrust Act (1914), which aimed to dismantle monopolistic practices that concentrated wealth and power in the hands of a few. These laws, championed by figures like Theodore Roosevelt, sought to level the economic playing field by promoting competition and preventing corporate abuses.

Labor movements also gained momentum during this period, driven by demands for fair wages, reasonable working hours, and safer conditions. Strikes such as the 1912 Lawrence Textile Strike underscored the growing unrest among industrial workers, while organizations like the American Federation of Labor (AFL) fought for collective bargaining rights. Progressive reformers viewed these efforts as essential to mitigating class tensions and promoting economic justice.

Social reformers, many of whom were women, played a pivotal role in pushing for change during this era. The women's suffrage movement, a cornerstone of Progressive Era reform, culminated in the ratification of the 19th Amendment in 1920, granting women the right to vote. This milestone not only expanded democratic participation but also symbolized a broader effort to address societal inequities and empower marginalized groups. However, these reforms were not without resistance. Business interests and conservative factions pushed back against increased government regulation and labor protections, fearing that such changes would disrupt traditional hierarchies and economic freedoms.

This tension between progress and resistance exemplifies a recurring theme in American history: efforts to expand rights and equality often deepen ideological divisions. The Progressive Era reforms, while transformative, highlighted emerging fault lines in political ideology—particularly over the role of government in

27

shaping society. These divides would become even more pronounced during the New Deal, as debates over federal intervention and economic policy reshaped the nation's political landscape. Together, the Progressive Era and New Deal reforms marked a critical shift in polarization, from regional disputes to ideological battles over class, governance, and the very meaning of democracy.

The Great Depression of the 1930s brought economic devastation on a scale never before seen in the United States, prompting a dramatic expansion of federal power under President Franklin D. Roosevelt's New Deal. Programs like the Works Progress Administration (WPA) and Social Security aimed to provide relief to millions of unemployed Americans, stabilize the economy, and prevent future crises. These policies represented a fundamental shift in the relationship between the federal government and the economy, with the state taking on a more active role in ensuring economic security.

While many Americans embraced the New Deal as a lifeline during a time of unprecedented hardship, conservatives viewed these programs as an overreach of federal authority. Critics argued that the expansion of government threatened individual freedoms and free-market capitalism. The Supreme Court initially struck down several New Deal measures, reflecting the polarized views on Roosevelt's policies. Although the administration ultimately prevailed in implementing its agenda, the ideological divide over government intervention became a defining feature of American politics.

The Progressive and New Deal eras laid the groundwork for modern debates about the role of government in tackling economic and social challenges. Efforts to regulate industry, expand labor protections, and establish social safety nets helped address some of the inequalities of industrial capitalism but also entrenched ideological polarization. The divide between those who view government as a vehicle for equality and those who see it as a threat to personal liberty became a defining feature of American politics.

As the 20th century progressed, this ideological tension

evolved into broader cultural and racial divides. The mid-20th century brought a new wave of transformative movements, from the Civil Rights Movement to feminist and anti-war activism, each challenging entrenched systems of inequality. While these movements made historic strides toward justice, they also intensified cultural polarization, reshaping political and social identities in ways that continue to influence the nation today. The debates of the Progressive and New Deal eras over equality and governance set the stage for the cultural and racial polarization that would define the post-World War II decades.

Civil Rights and Social Movements (1945–1980)

The post-World War II era ushered in sweeping social changes that reshaped the United States, tackling entrenched inequalities but also deepening cultural divides. This period saw the rise of transformative movements, from the Civil Rights Movement to second-wave feminism and anti-war protests, each confronting societal norms and challenging the status quo. While these movements achieved significant milestones, they also exposed and exacerbated existing tensions, laying the foundation for the "culture wars" that continue to shape American politics today.

The Civil Rights Movement of the 1950s and 1960s marked a turning point in the struggle for racial equality. Leaders like Martin Luther King Jr., Rosa Parks, and organizations such as the NAACP fought against systemic racism through protests, boycotts, and legal challenges. Landmark legislation, including the Civil Rights Act of 1964 and the Voting Rights Act of 1965, dismantled segregation and protected African Americans' voting rights. These achievements represented a hard-fought victory for justice, redefining the nation's commitment to equality.

However, the success of the Civil Rights Movement also triggered significant political realignment. Southern Democrats, known as Dixiecrats, strongly opposed civil rights legislation and began gravitating toward the Republican Party. This shift marked the beginning of a broader transformation in

American politics, as racial and cultural issues increasingly polarized voters along party lines. The Republican Party, adopting Richard Nixon's "Southern Strategy" in the late 1960s, appealed to disaffected white voters in the South, using racial resentment as a tool for political mobilization. This realignment solidified the racial polarization of American politics, with the South becoming a Republican stronghold.

The 1960s and 1970s witnessed a cultural revolution that expanded beyond racial equality to address gender and sexual liberation. Second-wave feminism emerged as a powerful force, advocating for workplace equality, reproductive rights, and the passage of the Equal Rights Amendment (ERA). While the ERA ultimately failed to gain ratification, the movement achieved major victories, such as Title IX of the Education Amendments Act of 1972, which prohibited sex-based discrimination in federally funded education programs.

One of the most polarizing moments of this era came with the Supreme Court's decision in Roe v. Wade (1973), which legalized abortion nationwide. This landmark ruling ignited a cultural firestorm, galvanizing religious and conservative groups and intensifying the broader backlash against progressive social change. Similarly, the LGBTQ+ rights movement gained momentum, with pivotal events like the 1969 Stonewall Riots challenging societal norms and advocating for equality. As debates over abortion, gender roles, and LGBTQ+ rights deepened cultural and religious divides, these tensions extended beyond personal identity to questions of national values. This polarization laid the groundwork for the ideological clashes that would erupt over the Vietnam War, as generational and political conflicts over authority and patriotism further fragmented the nation.

The Vietnam War became another flashpoint of division, sparking widespread protests throughout the 1960s and 1970s. Younger Americans, particularly college students, led anti-war demonstrations, questioning the morality and necessity of the conflict. Organizations like Students for a Democratic Society (SDS) and events such as the Kent State shootings in 1970 highlighted the intensity of these generational clashes. Many older Americans viewed the protests as unpatriotic and disrespectful, leading to a broader ideological divide over authority, national security, and individual rights.

The anti-war movement further fractured the nation, with public opinion deeply split over the government's role and decisions. This generational divide contributed to the growing perception of a cultural chasm between progressives advocating for change and conservatives defending traditional values.

By the end of this period, social issues had taken center stage in American politics, leading to what became known as the "culture wars." Racial equality, gender roles, sexual liberation, and generational differences fueled debates that reshaped the nation's political landscape. These divisions were not merely ideological but deeply personal, touching on identity, morality, and the nation's future. The polarization that emerged during this era set the stage for many of the cultural and political conflicts that continue to define American society.

And if I may, let me say this:

Human rights are not a finite resource, reserved for a select few—they are the foundation upon which we build a world where everyone belongs. My love for humanity is not limited by borders, identities, or histories; it is fueled by the belief that our differences are not divisions but intersections, places where we connect and grow stronger. Intersectionality is not just a framework. It is the heartbeat of justice, reminding us that no one is truly free until everyone is free. It beats for equality, for dignity, and for the unwavering belief that every person deserves to live without fear or oppression. It pulses through the struggles of the marginalized, the victories of the resilient, and the dreams of those who dare to hope for a better tomorrow.

I say this because learning about this era—the courage, the failures, and the triumphs—was one of the things that inspired me to write this book, to explore how we can bridge divides and move forward as one.

Living the Divide (1980-Present)

From 1980 to the present, the events shaping America's polarization are not "history" in the traditional sense—they are living, evolving realities. Unlike the Civil War or Reconstruction, which we examine through the lens of time and reflection, the dynamics of the past few decades are still unfolding, shaping the world we inhabit today. To call this period "history" is to imply a resolution, a sense of finality, and the clarity of hindsight, none of which exist in the polarized present.

This era represents the polarization we are actively experiencing, not something safely confined to the past. The Reagan Revolution, the rise of cable news, the War on Terror, social media, and the Trump presidency are all chapters in a story still being written. The outcomes of these events—whether they heal or fracture us further—remain uncertain.

By choosing not to write about this period as history, I emphasize the immediacy of the challenge. This is not a narrative we can simply read; it is one we must engage with, influence, and change. Our actions today will determine whether future generations view this time as a moment of failure or as the turning point when we decide to come together and confront polarization head-on.

Lessons Etched in History

As we reflect on the story of America's divisions, one truth becomes clear: polarization isn't a new phenomenon. It's as old as the nation itself. The very foundation of the United States was built on compromise and contradiction—on the promise of liberty paired with the reality of inequality. From these historical tensions, we see a pattern emerge: division is inevitable, but unity is possible when we confront our differences with purpose and resolve.

Throughout this chapter, we've explored how the nation's identity has been shaped by conflict and reconciliation. From the fierce debates of the Constitutional Convention to the bloody fields of the Civil War, from the sweeping changes of Reconstruction to the cultural upheavals of the Civil Rights Movement, each era reveals how division stems not only from competing interests but from differing visions of what America should be. These conflicts have tested the limits of our democracy, yet they also show us that progress is possible—even in the face of seemingly insurmountable divides.

However, the divisions we face today are uniquely challenging because polarization is no longer just a symptom of political disagreement—it has become a way of life. Unlike in previous eras, when periods of intense division were often followed by moments of national reflection and reconciliation, today's divides are reinforced by the very systems and routines that shape our daily lives. Where we live, the media we consume, the social circles we maintain, and even the brands we support are increasingly defined by our ideological identities. Polarization now extends beyond the halls of Congress or the pages of newspapers; it infiltrates the fabric of our personal and collective experiences, making it harder to recognize and address.

This entrenched polarization creates echo chambers that amplify division and hinder progress. In past conflicts, physical proximity to opposing viewpoints often forced engagement— neighbors, coworkers, and families lived with and learned from one another despite their differences. Today, the digital and cultural landscapes have made it easier than ever to isolate ourselves within ideological bubbles, where opposing views are not just unfamiliar but actively distrusted. This makes the work of unity more difficult, as the tools and habits we've developed to navigate the modern world often deepen divides rather than bridge them.

The pattern of division and reconciliation in American history shows us that progress is possible—but it also warns us that overcoming today's polarization will require unprecedented effort. Unlike in the past, we must confront a polarization that has deeply infiltrated our identities and daily lives, making unity more challenging than ever. Yet, as Alexander Hamilton urged in Federalist No. 1, this nation has been entrusted with a rare opportunity: to prove that societies can establish good government through "reflection and choice" rather than "accident and force."

To honor that vision, we must rise above the forces that seek to divide us, recognizing that the work of democracy is not just about preserving what we have but about building something better. We must rebuild not only our institutions but also the social bonds that connect us as a people. Progress is still within reach, but achieving it will demand a profound understanding of what divides us and the courage to challenge those divisions. If we fail, we risk falling short of the promise this country was founded on—that we can create a government and a society worthy of the ideals of liberty, equality, and unity. The choice is ours: to retreat into division or to rise together, making a better country not just for ourselves but for generations to come.

The Human Impact of Polarization

Polarization is a term often thrown around in modern discourse, yet its true meaning remains elusive. For many, it's a catch-all explanation for societal discord, from political gridlock to cultural rifts. But polarization is far more than mere disagreement—it's a process that deepens divides, hardens identities, and fuels animosity. In its wake, collaboration becomes a distant memory, replaced by hostility, mistrust, and an "us versus them" mentality that infects nearly every facet of society.

At its core, polarization is not just about opposing viewpoints. It's about the intensification of those views, turning ideological differences into unbridgeable chasms. It's what happens when political parties become tribes, debates turn into battles, and the other side is not just wrong but perceived as morally corrupt or even dangerous. This transformation erodes the foundations of democratic discourse, making compromise feel like defeat.

Yet, confusion about what polarization truly is often hampers efforts to address it. Many conflate it with healthy disagreement or dismiss it as a natural consequence of diverse societies. In reality, polarization extends beyond political partisanship, seeping into cultural debates, social relationships, and even personal choices like the brands we buy or the media we consume.

This chapter seeks to demystify polarization by exploring what it is—and what it is not. By disentangling the concept from common misconceptions, we can better understand its origins and effects, paving the way for strategies to mitigate its impact and rebuild a society where differences can coexist without tearing communities apart.

Polarization Is Not Just Disagreement

At first glance, polarization and disagreement might seem interchangeable, both involving opposing views and contested perspectives. However, while disagreement is an essential component of healthy democratic systems, polarization is a more insidious process that can undermine the very foundation of productive discourse. Understanding how the two are similar yet fundamentally different is key to addressing the challenges posed by polarization.

Disagreement, in its healthiest form, is a driver of innovation and progress. It allows individuals and groups to debate ideas, refine policies, and challenge the status quo. For instance, the U.S. Civil Rights Movement in the 1960s was marked by profound disagreements over racial equality and justice, reflecting the deep societal divides of the time. Activists advocating for civil rights clashed with defenders of segregation and systemic inequality. Yet, as we have learned, despite the high stakes and intense resistance, this era was notably less polarized in comparison to today, creating opportunities for dialogue and eventual progress. While I don't necessarily believe that peaceful protest is inherently superior to other forms of resistance, the movement's approach highlights how disagreement—when not entrenched in polarization—can lead to transformative change.

The Civil Rights Movement's success depended on the sacrifices of those who endured immense personal and collective suffering. Protesters faced violence, imprisonment, and even death, as in the case of activists like Medgar Evers and the young victims of the 16th Street Baptist Church bombing. These sacrifices were not just a response to disagreement but a testament to their willingness to bridge moral divides in pursuit of justice. Their courage forced the nation to confront its conscience and galvanized legislative achievements like the Civil Rights Act of 1964 and the Voting Rights Act of 1965.

However, the movement's constructive use of disagreement, compared to today's polarized climate, offers a key insight. Unlike the rigid, emotionally charged dynamics of polarization, disagreements of that era, though contentious, still left room for a shared vision of progress. Leaders like Dr. Martin Luther King Jr. framed their demands in universal terms of justice and equality, appealing to ideals that resonated across divides. This ability to articulate a common moral ground was instrumental in fostering eventual consensus.

Recognizing the sacrifices of the activists of that era reminds us that progress often comes at a great cost. It also highlights how less polarized contexts—where opponents, however staunch, are not entirely vilified—create opportunities for transformative change, even amidst profound disagreements. Today's polarized society could benefit from reflecting on this dynamic, where disagreement fueled progress rather than becoming an insurmountable divide.

Polarization, we must remember, takes disagreement to an extreme. It is characterized by entrenchment, emotional hostility, and the perception that the opposing side is not just wrong but morally flawed or dangerous. For example, the current debate over climate change policies often exemplifies polarization. Instead of discussing practical solutions, polarized factions frame the issue in moral absolutes: one side accuses the other of denying science and endangering the planet, while the other claims opponents are sabotaging economic progress and personal freedoms. These emotionally charged narratives make collaboration nearly impossible, as neither side is willing to concede any legitimacy to the other's concerns.

The difference lies in the underlying attitudes and dynamics. Disagreement respects the legitimacy of opposing viewpoints and values debate as a means to reach better outcomes. Polarization, however, thrives on dehumanization and distrust, escalating divisions to the point where compromise is seen as betrayal.

While polarization and disagreement can appear similar in their external manifestations, their deeper mechanics reveal a critical divergence. This distinction becomes even more pronounced when we consider another closely related concept: partisanship. Partisanship, like disagreement, is not inherently harmful, but when fused with polarization, it can exacerbate societal divides to dangerous levels. Understanding this interplay is vital to addressing the broader challenges of a polarized society.

Polarization Is *Not* Partisanship

Polarization extends far beyond mere disagreement; it reshapes how individuals perceive not just issues, but each other. When ideological divisions deepen, they create barriers to understanding and collaboration, influencing everything from personal relationships to national governance. This phenomenon is often conflated with partisanship, but the two concepts are also fundamentally different. While partisanship refers to loyalty to a specific political party, polarization refers to the growing distance and hostility between opposing ideological camps. Understanding this distinction is critical to addressing the challenges of modern American politics.

Partisanship, in its essence, is not inherently harmful. It reflects the natural diversity of opinions in a democratic society and serves as a vehicle for political competition. Healthy partisanship allows individuals to organize around shared values and policy goals, fostering debate and accountability. Political parties play an essential role in representing different constituencies, mobilizing voters, and shaping public policy.

As previously explored, the debates between Federalists and Anti-Federalists during America's founding illustrate how partisanship can drive constructive political dialogue. These debates, while intense, were rooted in a shared commitment to building a functional democracy. Partisanship, when balanced by norms of civility and compromise, can enrich democratic governance. However, as you should know by now, polarization represents a departure from this model. It transforms political competition into existential conflict, where opposing parties are not just rivals but enemies. This distinction is crucial to understanding why polarization is so corrosive to democracy.

Polarization is fundamentally about identity. Unlike partisanship, which is often tied to policy preferences or political ideology, polarization is rooted in how individuals perceive themselves and others. Political affiliation has become a core component of personal identity for many Americans, often intertwined with race, religion, geography, and culture. This phenomenon, known as "identity politics," has fueled the rise of what political scientist Lilliana Mason calls "mega-identities."

In Uncivil Agreement: How Politics Became Our Identity, Lilliana Mason unpacks a concept she calls "mega-identities," where political affiliation becomes intertwined with almost every facet of life—religion, lifestyle, even the brands we choose to buy. This merging of identities doesn't just reinforce political allegiances; it turns political disagreements into something deeply personal. Suddenly, a disagreement over tax policy isn't just about numbers—it feels like a challenge to who you are at your core.

You can see the impact of these mega-identities in the way Americans navigate their relationships. A study highlighted by UC Berkeley's Haas School of Business noted that in 1960, only 10% of parents expressed discomfort at the idea of their child marrying someone from the opposing political party. By 2010, that figure had climbed to 33%. Think about what that means. Political alignment, once just one part of someone's identity, now carries enough emotional weight to disrupt one of the most intimate and personal relationships in life. This trend reflects a seismic shift in how polarization shapes not just political discourse but the very fabric of our personal connections. It's no longer about policy disagreements; it's about viewing the other side as incompatible with your core values—and by extension, your family.

This deepening divide in personal relationships is not just anecdotal. From couples navigating political differences in their marriages to the growing epidemic of estrangement in families due to opposing political views, polarization is redefining how we relate to those closest to us. As noted in a Wall Street Journal piece, many married couples find themselves voting differently while struggling to reconcile those differences at home. Similarly, Time magazine has explored how political divisions contribute to family estrangements, turning political identity into a line that, for some, cannot be crossed.

Polarization becomes dangerous when it undermines democratic norms and institutions. In highly polarized societies, political opponents are often viewed as illegitimate or untrustworthy. This erosion of trust can lead to gridlock, as parties refuse to cooperate or compromise. It can also fuel anti-democratic behaviors, such as efforts to delegitimize election outcomes or suppress dissent.

Harvard political scientists Steven Levitsky and Daniel Ziblatt, in their book How Democracies Die, warn that extreme polarization creates a zero-sum environment where the goal is not to govern but to defeat the opposition at any cost. In such an environment, democratic norms—such as mutual tolerance and institutional forbearance—are often the first casualties

For example, the impeachment trials of recent U.S. presidents offer a stark illustration of how polarization can overshadow substantive debate. Rather than engaging deeply with the merits of the case, many legislators defaulted to voting along party lines, underscoring how polarization has eroded the capacity for objective deliberation. Sound familiar? It's the same pattern we see in countless aspects of public life today—important decisions reduced to partisan battles, where the outcome is often determined not by careful analysis but by which side has the numbers. This dynamic doesn't just stall progress; it weakens trust in the process itself, leaving many Americans questioning whether meaningful dialogue is even possible anymore.

In the summer of 1964, the halls of the United States Capitol buzzed with tension. The Civil Rights Act, a landmark piece of legislation aiming to end segregation and outlaw discrimination based on race, color, religion, sex, or national origin, had sparked fierce debate. The country was at a crossroads, with voices from every corner weighing in. On one side, there was resistance, even outright hostility, to the sweeping changes the bill proposed. On the other side, a determined coalition of lawmakers from both parties saw the moment as a moral imperative, an opportunity to redefine the nation's values.

Among them was Senator Everett Dirksen, a Republican from Illinois. A man of measured words and a commanding presence, Dirksen believed that America's strength lay in its ability to confront its deepest flaws. Though his party was divided, Dirksen stepped into the fray. He understood the stakes—not just politically, but historically. For weeks, he worked tirelessly to persuade his Republican colleagues to support the bill, often reminding them of the nation's founding ideals of equality and justice.

The opposition was formidable. Southern Democrats mounted a filibuster, determined to block the legislation at all costs. The filibuster stretched on for 60 days, an exhausting ordeal that tested the resolve of every senator. But Dirksen, alongside Democratic Senate Majority Leader Mike Mansfield, pushed forward. In one particularly dramatic moment, Dirksen addressed the Senate chamber, quoting Victor Hugo: "Stronger than all the armies is an idea whose time has come." His voice echoed through the room, carrying with it the weight of conviction and the promise of change.

Behind the scenes, Dirksen worked across the aisle, engaging in private negotiations and forging alliances that transcended party lines. He believed deeply in the power of compromise—not as a sign of weakness, but as a tool for progress. His efforts paid off. On June 10, 1964, the filibuster was broken with a 71-29 vote, paving the way for the bill's passage. Just weeks later, on July 2, President Lyndon B. Johnson signed the Civil Rights Act into law, marking a pivotal moment in American history.

This story of the Civil Rights Act is a testament to partisanship without polarization. Lawmakers held firmly to their party identities and ideological beliefs, but they didn't let those differences stand in the way of addressing a national crisis. Dirksen's role exemplifies what can happen when leaders prioritize the greater good over partisan victories. It's a reminder that even in moments of deep division, cooperation and courage can bring about transformative change.

Polarization is not the same as partisanship and conflating the two obscures the root causes of our divisions. Healthy partisanship, when grounded in respect and a shared commitment to democratic principles, fuels competition and accountability. Polarization, on the other hand, represents a deeper societal rift— one that undermines trust, civility, and the very mechanisms that allow us to govern effectively.

This is a point we keep coming back to in this book because it cannot be overstated: polarization rips us apart. It tears at the fabric of our democracy, turning neighbors into enemies and disagreements into existential threats. If there's one thing I want you to take away from this discussion, it's the recognition of how destructive polarization is and how urgently we need to confront it.

Understanding the difference between polarization and partisanship is a critical step toward building a healthier political culture. By addressing the identity-driven forces that fuel polarization and rediscovering the potential for partisanship to coexist with collaboration, we can begin to rebuild our social and political systems. But to truly tackle polarization, we need to understand why the confusion between these concepts persists— how it has taken hold in our collective consciousness and what it says about the current state of our democracy. That is the focus of the next section.

Why the Confusion Persists

Imagine this: A young woman walks into her childhood home for Thanksgiving dinner. The scent of roasted turkey fills the air, and her mother greets her with a warm smile. But her stomach churns because she knows what's coming. She knows the conversation will eventually veer into politics, and the familiar tension will thicken the air. Her uncle will make a comment she can't let go, and her father will shake his head, muttering something under his breath. She used to love these gatherings, but now they feel like walking into a battlefield.

This is what polarization does. It doesn't just live in debates or rallies or news headlines. It creeps into our most sacred spaces—our families, our friendships, our communities—and turns them into war zones. The confusion between polarization and simple political disagreement or partisanship persists because its impact feels so personal. It feels like something that shouldn't be happening, like a betrayal of the people we thought we knew.

Take, for instance, the story of two lifelong friends. They grew up together, shared everything, and were closer than siblings. But one day, during a casual conversation, something snapped. One friend couldn't believe the other supported a particular candidate, and the other was just as incredulous about their friend's stance on an issue. What began as a disagreement turned into silence, and that silence grew into distance. They stopped texting. They stopped calling. Now, they avoid each other entirely, each convinced that the other is no longer the person they thought they knew.

The human impact of polarization isn't just ideological—it's deeply emotional. It's the feeling of alienation when someone you love no longer feels like a safe space. It's the heartbreak of realizing that a shared history doesn't necessarily mean a shared future. And it's the confusion of wondering how a difference in perspective could cause such a profound rupture.

Part of the reason this confusion persists is that polarization weaponizes our sense of identity. Imagine a mother and son who used to talk every day. The son moves away, starts working in a city that feels worlds apart from his rural hometown. His experiences shape his worldview, just as his mother's life shapes hers. Over time, their conversations shift. The warmth they once shared starts to cool. The mother feels judged by her son's new beliefs, while the son feels stifled by what he perceives as her unwillingness to change. Neither can see the other without the lens of their political identities coloring the view.

It's not just the disagreements that hurt—it's the loss of connection. A mother and son who love each other now talk past each other, their conversations becoming minefields. How did it get like this? How can they find their way back? The confusion lies in believing this is simply political when, in reality, it's a profound disruption of how we see one another as human beings.

Polarization also isolates us. Imagine being at a community event, a barbecue in a local park. You used to feel comfortable striking up a conversation with anyone, regardless of their political affiliation. But now, there's hesitation. You wonder, What if they're one of those people? The fear of being judged—or worse, attacked—keeps you silent. Over time, that silence becomes habit, and the habit becomes a wall. You stop engaging. You stop connecting.

This isolation isn't just social; it's emotional. It's the ache of feeling alone even when you're surrounded by people. It's the slow realization that the bonds you once took for granted have frayed, and you don't know how to repair them.

Polarization makes us question the very foundations of our relationships. A husband and wife who've built a life together suddenly find themselves at odds. Every conversation feels like a debate. Every disagreement feels like a referendum on their values. They wonder, How can we love each other if we see the world so differently?

It's not the politics that break them—it's the feeling of being unseen, unheard, misunderstood. Polarization magnifies these feelings, turning everyday frustrations into insurmountable barriers. It tells us that compromise is impossible and that understanding is weakness.

Even strangers aren't immune. Think about the person you pass on the street wearing a T-shirt or a hat that signals their political beliefs. Maybe you feel a pang of anger or a surge of judgment. Maybe you cross the street or avoid making eye contact. You don't know them. You don't know their story. But polarization convinces you that you do. It tells you that they are your enemy, even though they're just a human being, walking through life with the same fears and hopes as you.

The human cost of this confusion is staggering. It's families who no longer gather. It's friendships that quietly dissolve. It's communities that grow colder, more suspicious, less willing to engage. And it's the internal toll—anxiety, frustration, grief— that we carry as we navigate a world that feels more divided with each passing day.

This isn't just about politics. It's about trust. It's about connection. It's about the stories we tell ourselves about who we are and who others are. And until we confront the way polarization distorts those stories, the confusion will persist.

Polarization doesn't just tear us apart; it convinces us that the tearing is inevitable. It tells us that our differences are too great, our divides too wide, our disagreements too deep. But this isn't true. The confusion between polarization and partisanship, or polarization and disagreement, is a symptom of something deeper—a longing for connection that feels increasingly out of reach.

We have to recognize this for what it is: a crisis not of politics, but of humanity. Only then can we begin to rebuild the relationships, the communities, and the trust that polarization has taken from us.

Destructive Division Vs. Healthy Debate

Conflict is inevitable in any society. It arises wherever there are divergent views, competing interests, or differing values. But the way we handle conflict determines whether it serves as a catalyst for growth or as a force that fractures relationships, communities, and even entire nations. The distinction between destructive division and healthy debate lies not in the presence of disagreement but in how that disagreement is expressed and resolved.

Destructive division and healthy debate both arise from differences, but they operate in entirely different frameworks. One sees differences as irreconcilable threats; the other views them as opportunities for dialogue, growth, and even innovation. To move forward, we must critically examine the forces that lead us into destructive division and explore how to cultivate spaces for healthy debate.

Destructive division doesn't emerge in a vacuum—it's built incrementally through patterns of mistrust, fear, and dehumanization. At its core, destructive division happens when disagreements escalate into battles of identity rather than arguments about ideas.

Identity plays a key role here. In polarized environments, disagreements become existential. People feel that to compromise on a position or even engage in dialogue risks undermining their very sense of self. This leads to zero-sum thinking—where one side's gain is perceived as the other side's loss. In such a mindset, opponents are not just wrong; they are dangerous, corrupt, or irredeemably flawed.

This is where destructive division takes hold. Instead of addressing the issue at hand, debates devolve into personal attacks and efforts to invalidate the other side's legitimacy. Social media amplifies these tendencies, rewarding performative outrage and polarizing rhetoric with likes, shares, and algorithmic reinforcement. Over time, the echo chambers we inhabit reinforce these divisions, hardening our positions and making dialogue feel futile.

But destructive division is not only harmful to political or social systems—it also has profound personal consequences. Families stop speaking to one another. Friendships dissolve. Communities fracture into insular subgroups, unable to collaborate even on shared challenges. In these moments, the price of division is not just ideological—it's human.

Healthy debate operates in a fundamentally different way. It acknowledges the reality of conflict but frames it as a constructive force. In this framework, disagreements are not threats to identity but invitations to explore differences, refine perspectives, and find common ground.

The foundation of healthy debate is mutual respect. This does not mean agreement or even approval of another's viewpoint—it means valuing the person behind the argument and approaching their ideas with a willingness to understand rather than invalidate. Respect creates space for curiosity, which is another cornerstone of healthy debate.

Curiosity shifts the focus from "How can I prove them wrong?" to "What can I learn from their perspective?" It encourages participants to ask questions like:

o   What values are driving this person's position?
o   What assumptions might I be making about their argument?
o   How might their experiences have shaped their beliefs?

When debate is approached with curiosity, the goal shifts from victory to understanding. This does not mean abandoning conviction or avoiding tough questions. On the contrary, healthy debate often involves strong, passionate arguments. But those arguments are presented in good faith, with the understanding that disagreement is not a personal attack but a natural byproduct of diversity.

History offers a stark contrast between the outcomes of destructive division and healthy debate. Consider the Constitutional Convention of 1787. Delegates from the newly independent states faced enormous disagreements over representation, federal power, and the institution of slavery. These were not trivial issues; they cut to the core of the nation's identity and future.

Yet, despite their differences, the delegates managed to engage in what we would now call healthy debate. Compromises were forged—not always perfectly, but with a recognition that collaboration was necessary to create a functional union. The Constitution that emerged was a testament to the power of dialogue and negotiation in the face of profound disagreement.

Now contrast this with the period leading up to the Civil War. The divisions between the North and South over slavery and state sovereignty were equally fundamental, but this time, the ability to engage in debate was lost. Communication broke down, trust evaporated, and positions became so entrenched that dialogue was no longer possible. The result was catastrophic conflict—a failure not just of policy but of the human ability to manage disagreement.

These examples illustrate the stakes of how we engage with conflict. Healthy debate builds systems and relationships; destructive division tears them apart.

At the heart of both destructive division and healthy debate lies emotional infrastructure—the way we regulate emotions, manage fear, and build trust in the face of conflict. Destructive division often takes root because fear overrides our ability to engage constructively. Fear narrows our focus, heightens our defensiveness, and encourages us to see others as threats.

To counteract this, healthy debate relies on emotional intelligence. This involves:

- **Self-awareness:** Recognizing when emotions like anger or defensiveness are clouding judgment.
- **Empathy:** Understanding the emotions and motivations of others without necessarily agreeing with them.
- **Emotional Regulation:** Managing one's emotional reactions to remain composed and focused on the issue at hand.

.

Consider a workplace disagreement over a major project decision. In a setting marked by destructive division, this disagreement might escalate into personal rivalries or a toxic atmosphere where trust is eroded. However, in a setting where emotional intelligence is prioritized, the disagreement becomes an opportunity for team members to share perspectives, challenge assumptions, and refine their approach collectively. The difference lies in how emotions are managed and how participants view one another—as collaborators or as adversaries.

A major barrier to healthy debate is the erosion of trust. Trust, once broken, is difficult to rebuild, but it is not impossible. One way to restore trust is through consistency—showing through actions, not just words, that dialogue is being approached in good faith.

Another approach is to find shared values, even in polarized environments. For example, two people on opposite sides of a policy debate might both care deeply about fairness or safety, even if they disagree on how to achieve those outcomes. Acknowledging these shared values can create a foundation for dialogue, even in the midst of disagreement.

The distinction between destructive division and healthy debate isn't just an abstract concept—it's a defining challenge of our time, one that touches every aspect of our lives. The way we handle disagreement has profound implications for our relationships, our communities, and the future of our society. The key truth is this: disagreement is not the problem. The problem is how we engage with it. And the solution starts with you.

Healthy debate doesn't happen by accident. It requires effort—sometimes more effort than we think we're capable of. It demands emotional intelligence, respect, and a willingness to truly listen, even when the words are hard to hear. But the rewards are worth it. When we choose healthy debate, we create space for stronger relationships, innovative solutions, and a society built on mutual trust and resilience.

Destructive division, on the other hand, thrives on fear and mistrust. It promises the illusion of quick victories—the satisfaction of proving someone wrong, the comfort of retreating into your own perspective. But what it leaves behind is the wreckage of broken relationships, fractured communities, and stagnant systems incapable of solving the challenges we face.

You have a choice. Every disagreement, every conversation, every conflict is an opportunity to decide how you will engage. Will you see the person across from you as a fellow human with a perspective shaped by their unique experiences? Or will you dismiss them as an obstacle to be defeated? Will you approach disagreements with curiosity and humility, or will you let defensiveness and fear take the lead?

Conflict is inevitable, but division is not. Healthy debate doesn't mean backing down or compromising your values—it means channeling disagreement into a force for progress. It means being brave enough to build bridges instead of burning them, to seek understanding instead of validation, and to find common ground even when it feels impossibly far away.

The way you engage with conflict today will shape the relationships, communities, and systems of tomorrow. So, take a stand—not just for your beliefs, but for the integrity of the debate itself. Be the person who listens when others shout, who seeks connection when others withdraw, and who challenges division wherever it appears.

This isn't just about them; it's about you. Your choices matter. Your conversations matter. Together, we can transform disagreement from a source of division into a foundation for growth. But it starts with a simple, powerful decision: Choose to debate with purpose. Choose to engage with empathy. Choose to build a better future.

The Grand Vision

When I started writing this book, I told myself I wouldn't make it about me. This isn't my story—it's ours. It's about the choices we've made as humans, the paths we've taken, and the ways we've stumbled, struggled, and tried to make sense of it all. But as I sit here writing this section, I realize I owe you something personal. Not just because you've taken the time to read this far— though I'm deeply grateful that you have—but because this book exists for a reason, and that reason is deeply tied to how I see the world and how I see you.

Let me start with this: thank you. Thank you for finishing this introduction to the topic of polarization. Thank you for being willing to explore something that is often painful and uncomfortable to confront. By reaching this point, you've already done something so many people won't—taken the time to question, to reflect, and to consider the possibility of something better.

I wrote this book because I believe in us. I believe in humans, even when we make it so hard to. We are capable of extraordinary things. We've reached into the cosmos, mapped the mysteries of DNA, and built civilizations from the ground up. But we're also capable of immense destruction. War, death, pain—these things aren't inevitable. They're choices we keep making, over and over, as if we've learned nothing from the countless times they've torn us apart.

It breaks my heart. Truly, it does. Because when I think about the suffering we've inflicted on one another—the needless cruelty, the fear, the divisions—it feels so senseless. And it's not just the big things like wars or genocides. It's the little things too: the relationships we've severed, the love we've withheld, the understanding we've refused to extend. These moments add up. They create a world where we spend more time hurting one another than helping.

But here's the thing: I don't believe it has to be this way. I believe humans could be so much better, so much further along than we are now. Think about what we could have achieved already if we had just worked together. Disease eradicated. Poverty eliminated. Peace maintained. There's so much brilliance in us—so much creativity, resilience, and hope. And yet, we've squandered it on things like greed, pride, and power.

I don't write this to make you feel bad. I write it because I love you. Yes, you—the reader holding this book in your hands. I don't know your story, your struggles, or your dreams, but I know you're human, and that means I love you in the way that we are meant to love one another: fully, unapologetically, and without condition.

You are part of the reason I wrote this book. Because I see so much potential in you—in all of us. I see the ways we could rise above the divisions we've created, the pain we've inflicted, and the mistakes we keep repeating. I see a future where we don't just survive, but thrive. And I believe that future is possible, not in some distant utopia, but here and now, in this lifetime.

I know it's hard to imagine. We've been so conditioned to believe that the world is irreparably broken, that people are inherently selfish, that conflict is unavoidable. But I don't buy it. I've seen too many moments of kindness, too many acts of courage, and too many flashes of brilliance to believe that this is all we're capable of.

That's why I'm writing this book. Because I want us to stop settling for less than what we could be. I want us to stop tearing each other apart and start building something together. I want us to look at the pain and suffering in the world—not just acknowledge it, but do something about it.

And yes, I know that sounds idealistic. I know people will say, "That's just the way things are." But I don't accept that. I can't. Because every time I think about the wars we've fought, the lives we've lost, the opportunities we've squandered, I feel this ache in my chest—a mix of grief and frustration and love.

Love for what we could be. Love for the brilliance I know exists in each of us. Love for the possibility that we can get this right, even if it takes longer than it should.

I believe we are capable of so much more than we give ourselves credit for. And yes, we've made silly, ridiculous, heartbreaking mistakes. But we've also done incredible things. We've loved deeply. We've built communities. We've overcome odds that seemed impossible. And we can do it again.

I'm writing this because I believe in a vision of humanity that rises above its worst instincts. A vision where we learn to live with our differences instead of letting them divide us. A vision where we recognize that the things that connect us—our shared humanity, our shared planet, our shared future—are infinitely more important than the things that separate us.

This isn't about pretending we're all the same or glossing over real problems. It's about finding ways to address those problems together, not as enemies, but as allies. It's about realizing that healthy debate can strengthen us, that empathy can transform us, and that collaboration can propel us further than any of us could go alone.

So, what comes next in this book? The final section is where I'll outline what I call The Grand Vision. It's not a blueprint or a step-by-step guide—it's a call to action. A way of thinking about the world that challenges us to be better, to reach higher, and to leave behind the divisions that have held us back for so long.

This vision isn't mine alone. It's one we must create together. It's a vision rooted in love, not fear; in possibility, not despair. It's a vision that asks each of us to step up and play our part, no matter how small.

But before we get there, I need you to know this: I believe in you. I believe in us. I believe that we can rise above the noise, the fear, the pain, and the hate. I believe that we can create a world where polarization isn't the norm, where compassion is stronger than division, and where we finally live up to the potential that's been inside us all along.

This book is my way of saying I love you, even when we've stumbled, even when we've hurt one another, even when we've lost our way. Because despite everything, I believe in the future we can create together. And I hope, by the end of this book, you will too.

Part II: The Forces Driving Polarization

"Peace cannot be kept by force; it can only be achieved by understanding."
- Albert Einstein, 1930

Political Polarization

Polarization has become a defining characteristic of modern society, touching every facet of life from the way we govern to how we interact in our communities. Part II of this book, Understanding Polarization, examines the roots, manifestations, and consequences of polarization through four key sections: Political Polarization, Media and Technology, Economic Inequality, and Cultural and Social Divides. Together, these sections provide a comprehensive framework for understanding how polarization shapes our world today—and what we can do about it.

In this first chapter, Political Polarization, we will focus on one of the most visible and impactful forms of polarization: the deepening divide in our political systems, ideologies, and governance. Political polarization isn't simply about policy differences; it is about the transformation of disagreement into division, often with far-reaching consequences for society as a whole.

Political polarization is not just a feature of contemporary politics; it is one of its defining challenges. At its core, political polarization refers to the growing ideological, emotional, and social divide between opposing political groups. This divide is characterized by an increasingly rigid alignment along partisan lines, where compromise and collaboration become rare, and hostility between groups becomes the norm.

This isn't just a theoretical issue; it is a lived reality. We see it in the way legislative bodies struggle to pass even the most basic measures, in the way political opponents are demonized as enemies, and in the way political affiliation has seeped into the most personal aspects of our lives. Understanding political polarization is essential because it has profound implications—not just for governance, but for the health of our democracy and the cohesion of our society

Defining Political Polarization

At its simplest, political polarization refers to the process by which individuals, groups, and institutions become more ideologically divided along political lines. It is important to distinguish between two types of polarization:

- o **Ideological Polarization:** This occurs when the political spectrum stretches, with individuals or parties moving toward the extremes. The center ground shrinks, and compromise becomes less likely.
- o **Affective Polarization:** This refers to the emotional and social divide between groups. People don't just disagree on issues; they actively dislike and distrust those who hold opposing views.

While ideological polarization is rooted in policy disagreements, affective polarization turns politics into a battle of identity. It shifts the focus from *what we believe* to *who we are*—and, by extension, *who we are against*. This change makes political divisions deeply personal, fueling distrust and hostility that reach far beyond the issues themselves.

Polarization isn't just a buzzword tossed around in the news or an abstract concept debated by political analysts. It's a force that quietly—and sometimes loudly—reshapes the way we govern, the way we live, and the way we connect with each other. The impacts aren't confined to political arenas; they ripple into homes, communities, and the very institutions we depend on. Let me walk you through why political polarization matters and why understanding its consequences is so important.

Imagine you're watching a football game, and both teams refuse to play unless they can control the scoreboard. That's what modern governance often feels like. In today's polarized political climate, compromise isn't just rare—it's often treated as treason. Lawmakers are rewarded for sticking to their ideological corners, even if it means nothing gets done.

Take the repeated deadlock over immigration reform. Dreamers—young people brought to the U.S. as children—have lived in limbo for years, caught in the crossfire of partisan battles. Both Democrats and Republicans have expressed interest in addressing their legal status, but no meaningful legislation has materialized. Why? Because even the idea of working across the aisle on such a charged issue is politically risky. Each side fears backlash from their base more than the consequences of inaction.

It's not just immigration. Climate change legislation, healthcare reform, and infrastructure improvements have all stalled for the same reasons. This isn't just frustrating—it's dangerous. The world doesn't pause for gridlock. Issues like rising temperatures, crumbling bridges, or spiraling healthcare costs demand action, but polarization makes meaningful progress feel like a distant dream.

And here's the kicker: this dysfunction erodes trust in government itself. According to Pew Research Center, trust in the federal government has been near historic lows for over a decade. People lose faith in the system when it seems incapable of solving problems. That disillusionment creates a feedback loop, where disengaged citizens feel disconnected, further amplifying the very polarization that paralyzed governance in the first place.

Polarization doesn't just make it hard to pass laws—it shakes the foundation of democracy itself. Think of democratic norms as unwritten agreements: respect for the rule of law, trust in elections, and faith in the impartiality of institutions. Polarization chips away at those agreements, turning them into weapons for partisan gain.

Take the U.S. Supreme Court. Once widely respected as an impartial arbiter of justice, it's now viewed by many as a political tool. After the court's decision in *Dobbs v. Jackson Women's Health Organization* overturned *Roe v. Wade*, public confidence in the institution plummeted to record lows. Whether you agree or disagree with the ruling, the fallout reveals something deeper: people no longer trust the court to act independently of politics.

It's not just the courts. Think about the electoral system itself. The 2020 presidential election was one of the most secure in U.S. history, according to federal and state election officials. Yet misinformation about voter fraud ran rampant, culminating in the January 6, 2021, Capitol riot. When trust in elections erodes, the consequences are dire. Democracy depends on the peaceful transfer of power, and when that trust falters, the entire system is at risk.

These aren't just cracks in the foundation—they're signs that the foundation itself is under strain. Once democratic norms are broken, they're incredibly hard to rebuild.

The most chilling consequence of polarization is its potential to spark violence—not just between individuals, but also systemic violence against marginalized groups. When opponents are seen not merely as adversaries but as existential threats, this mindset creates a dangerous justification for extreme actions. Polarization doesn't just pit "us" against "them"; it dehumanizes entire groups, making violence against them seem acceptable—or even necessary.

Consider the events of January 6, 2021, when a mob stormed the U.S. Capitol in an attempt to overturn the presidential election results. What began as a rally devolved into an insurrection, fueled by conspiracy theories and partisan distrust. The attack left a deep scar on American democracy, highlighting just how fragile it can be in the face of unchecked polarization. But beyond the immediate physical violence, the events of January 6 revealed the systemic dangers of political division: a willingness to undermine democratic institutions, spread misinformation, and disregard the rule of law.

This wasn't an isolated incident. In 2022, an intruder broke into the home of then-Speaker Nancy Pelosi, attacking her husband with a hammer. The assailant admitted he was motivated by political grievances rooted in conspiracy theories, specifically targeting Pelosi due to her prominent role in American politics. These attacks, both physical and symbolic, show how polarization fosters a climate where political leaders and their families become targets of hate-fueled violence.

Beyond high-profile cases, the systemic nature of violence becomes clear when examining hate crimes, which often rise in polarized environments. For example, the 2018 Tree of Life Synagogue shooting in Pittsburgh—the deadliest antisemitic attack in U.S. history—was fueled by conspiracy theories about immigrants and Jewish people. The shooter's beliefs were rooted in polarized, extremist rhetoric that portrayed certain groups as threats to American values and security. According to the FBI, hate crimes in the U.S. have been steadily increasing, with a 12% rise reported from 2020 to 2021 alone.

Polarization intensifies systemic violence by embedding distrust and hostility within institutions, communities, and rhetoric. This violence often disproportionately affects marginalized groups, but its reach extends to a wide range of populations, including white poor Americans, whose struggles are frequently exploited and politicized.

For example, the rise of anti-LGBTQ+ legislation in certain states has coincided with a surge in targeted violence against LGBTQ+ individuals. Transgender Americans, in particular, have faced increasing physical and rhetorical attacks as political debates about gender identity become more polarized. A 2023 report by the Human Rights Campaign found that anti-LGBTQ+ rhetoric has contributed to a rise in fatal violence, with at least 38 transgender or gender-nonconforming individuals murdered in the U.S. that year alone. The link between political rhetoric and real-world harm is undeniable: when leaders and media figures portray certain groups as threats to societal values, it creates a climate where systemic and physical violence feels justified.

Similarly, systemic violence against immigrants has been exacerbated by polarized narratives portraying them as criminals or invaders. In 2019, a mass shooting in El Paso, Texas, targeted Hispanic individuals, leaving 23 dead. The shooter explicitly cited fears of a "Hispanic invasion" in a manifesto, echoing language often used in polarized political discourse. Such narratives, amplified by partisan media and social platforms, not only dehumanize but also incite harm.

But the impacts of polarization-fueled systemic violence are not confined to marginalized communities. White poor Americans, often struggling with economic disenfranchisement, are also caught in the crosshairs of polarizing rhetoric. Instead of receiving meaningful support for structural challenges such as job loss, opioid addiction, and decaying infrastructure, they are frequently used as symbols in a broader culture war. Politicians and media figures on all sides frame their struggles either as evidence of national decline or as a contrast to the challenges faced by other groups, perpetuating resentment and division.

This resentment often manifests as self-directed violence or harmful behavior within their own communities. Regions hardest hit by deindustrialization and economic decline—especially rural areas populated predominantly by poor white Americans—frequently experience elevated rates of suicide, substance abuse, and domestic violence. The opioid epidemic has been particularly devastating. In 2022, opioid-related deaths reached record highs, with approximately 82,000 fatalities nationwide. Rural white Americans, already facing economic disenfranchisement and limited access to healthcare, continue to be disproportionately affected by this crisis.

These communities are often left out of national discourse, their struggles overshadowed by broader political narratives. This neglect not only alienates these populations but also exacerbates their vulnerabilities, leaving them to grapple with systemic challenges largely in isolation. Addressing these crises requires not just policy solutions but also a broader acknowledgment of their plight within the cultural and political conversations shaping the nation.

The intersection of polarization and systemic violence lies in its ability to exploit and deepen vulnerabilities across different demographics. Marginalized groups are targeted for their identities, while economically disadvantaged populations, including poor white Americans, are targeted through neglect and manipulation. In both cases, polarization uses these groups as pawns in a larger narrative of division, eroding trust and solidarity across society.

Understanding these dynamics is crucial as we turn to the broader trends that fuel modern polarization. In the next section, Modern-Day Trends in Polarization, we'll delve into the key forces driving these divides, including geography, economic inequality, and cultural shifts. These factors not only shape how polarization takes root but also determine how it spreads and intensifies throughout the United States. By unpacking these interconnected influences, we can better understand the root causes of systemic violence and begin to envision a path toward a society that prioritizes equity, empathy, and unity over division.

Modern-Day Trends in Polarization

Polarization often paints groups as adversaries, dividing people along lines of geography, race, class, or ideology. Yet beneath these divisions lies a shared truth: many of these groups are grappling with the same systemic challenges. Whether urban or rural, Black or white, college-educated or not, the issues they face—economic inequality, lack of access to resources, and distrust in institutions—are often strikingly similar. Understanding the trends that shape modern polarization isn't just about identifying divisions; it's about recognizing the common ground that could bring people together.

One of the most visible trends in modern polarization is the divide between urban and rural areas. Cities overwhelmingly lean Democratic, while rural areas strongly support Republicans. Suburban regions, once politically mixed, are now increasingly polarized depending on their proximity to cities or rural areas.

This divide is often framed as an irreconcilable cultural clash, but the reality is more nuanced. Urban areas, with their diversity and concentration of industries like technology and finance, tend to prioritize progressive policies on issues like climate change and social justice. Rural areas, facing economic struggles tied to agriculture, mining, and manufacturing, often feel left behind by these priorities.

However, beneath these surface-level differences, the challenges faced by urban and rural communities are deeply interconnected. Both struggle with rising housing costs, access to quality education, and economic instability. Rural areas may see job losses due to factory closures, while urban residents face gentrification and skyrocketing rents. These are two sides of the same coin, yet polarization frames them as competing narratives.

For example, rural voters may feel that urban policies on renewable energy ignore their economic realities, while urban voters may see rural resistance as a refusal to address global crises. In truth, both groups could benefit from comprehensive solutions that prioritize sustainable energy development alongside rural economic investment. Recognizing these shared interests is key to bridging the geographic divide.

Age, race, and education levels are significant drivers of polarization, but these divisions also obscure common struggles. Younger generations, such as Millennials and Gen Z, tend to lean Democratic, advocating for progressive policies on climate action, racial justice, and healthcare. Older generations, particularly Baby Boomers, often lean Republican, prioritizing economic conservatism and traditional values.

Race further complicates this picture. Nonwhite voters, particularly Black, Hispanic, and Asian Americans, overwhelmingly support the Democratic Party, while white voters, especially those without a college degree, are more likely to align with Republicans. Education, meanwhile, plays a decisive role: college-educated voters increasingly lean Democratic, while non-college-educated voters often support Republicans

At first glance, these differences seem insurmountable, but the underlying issues affecting these groups often overlap. Young voters, regardless of race or education, are increasingly burdened by student debt, limited job opportunities, and unaffordable housing. Older generations, meanwhile, face rising healthcare costs, dwindling retirement savings, and fears of being left behind in a rapidly changing economy.

Similarly, while race and education level influence voting patterns, economic insecurity transcends these divides. A low-income Black family in an urban center and a poor white family in a rural town both face systemic barriers to upward mobility. Yet polarization pits these groups against each other, framing their struggles as competing interests rather than shared challenges.

The political narratives that exploit these divisions distract from the systemic issues that affect everyone. Instead of addressing economic inequality or healthcare access, polarization encourages blame and resentment between groups that should be allies. Bridging these demographic divides requires reframing these shared struggles as opportunities for collaboration rather than competition.

.Economic inequality is a central force in modern polarization. Over the past several decades, the wealth gap in the United States has widened dramatically, creating stark differences in access to education, healthcare, and opportunities. These disparities often manifest as political divisions, with wealthier, urban populations prioritizing issues like climate change, while economically struggling rural and working-class communities focus on immediate concerns like jobs and healthcare.

However, this framing ignores the fact that economic inequality affects all demographics. Rural white Americans may face job losses due to factory closures, but urban Black and Hispanic Americans disproportionately experience low wages, housing insecurity, and lack of access to healthcare. Both groups are caught in systems that prioritize corporate profits over community well-being, yet polarization directs their frustrations toward each other rather than the root causes.

For example, policies like raising the minimum wage or expanding healthcare access would benefit both rural and urban communities. However, these policies are often framed as partisan issues, alienating groups that could otherwise find common ground. Instead of addressing these systemic challenges collectively, polarization fosters resentment, with each side believing their struggles are unique or overlooked.

The COVID-19 pandemic underscored these shared vulnerabilities. While remote work allowed some professionals to maintain financial stability, low-income workers—many in rural and urban service industries—faced job losses, unsafe working conditions, and inadequate healthcare access. These shared experiences highlight the potential for unity in addressing economic inequality, but polarization continues to obscure this commonality.

It should be noted that modern media plays a powerful role in deepening polarization by shaping how people consume and process information. Social media platforms like Facebook and YouTube often amplify sensational or divisive content through algorithms, creating echo chambers where users are primarily exposed to viewpoints that reinforce their existing beliefs. Traditional media outlets, such as Fox News and MSNBC, contribute to this divide by catering to ideological audiences and framing issues like immigration or economic policy in ways that align with their viewers' biases. This fragmentation not only entrenches divisions but also prevents groups with shared struggles—such as poor rural whites and low-income urban Black Americans—from recognizing their common interests. Generational differences in media consumption add another layer, with younger people favoring platforms like TikTok while older generations rely on cable news or newspapers. These dynamics, which foster mistrust and isolation, will be explored in greater depth in a later chapter on the influence of media and technology on polarization.

While geography, demographics, economics, and media are often framed as sources of division, they also reveal opportunities for unity. The urban-rural divide may seem insurmountable, but both areas struggle with economic insecurity, housing shortages, and lack of healthcare access. Similarly, demographic divides around race, age, and education often obscure shared challenges like student debt, stagnant wages, and systemic inequality.

Polarization thrives on narratives that pit these groups against each other, but the truth is that many of these struggles are interconnected. Recognizing these commonalities is the first step toward building bridges and fostering collaboration.

In the next section, *The Role of Institutions*, we'll examine how structural factors within governance, such as gerrymandering and legislative dysfunction, contribute to polarization. Understanding these systemic forces is critical to dismantling the barriers that prevent unity and addressing the root causes of division. By shifting the focus from what divides us to what connects us, we can begin to envision a society that prioritizes equity, empathy, and shared progress.

The Role of Institutions

Political polarization is often seen as a product of societal attitudes and media influence, but its roots are deeply intertwined with the very institutions that structure governance. Institutions shape the rules of engagement in politics, and over time, many have evolved to reinforce division rather than bridge it. From gerrymandering and primary elections to judicial decisions and the erosion of bipartisan norms, this section examines how institutions contribute to polarization and explores how they might be reformed to promote greater unity.

Gerrymandering, the practice of drawing electoral district boundaries to favor one party, plays a critical role in modern polarization. By creating "safe" districts, where one party is virtually guaranteed to win, gerrymandering reduces competition and allows candidates to appeal to their party's base without considering the broader electorate.

In these districts, the real contest often occurs during the primaries rather than the general election. This dynamic encourages candidates to adopt more extreme ideological positions to win over their party's most active and committed voters. For instance, a Republican candidate in a heavily gerrymandered district might feel pressure to oppose any compromise on gun control, while a Democrat in a similarly skewed district might face backlash for supporting moderate reforms to healthcare.

The creation of "safe" electoral districts through gerrymandering significantly exacerbates ideological polarization within legislative bodies. In these districts, representatives have little incentive to collaborate across party lines, as their primary electoral threat comes from more extreme challengers within their own party rather than from the opposing party. This dynamic encourages the election of candidates with more ideologically rigid positions, reducing the likelihood of bipartisan cooperation.

A 2023 analysis by the Brennan Center for Justice highlights the impact of redistricting on electoral competitiveness. The report notes that while independent commissions were responsible for drawing only 19% of congressional districts, they accounted for 41% of the districts rated as toss-ups in the 2024 elections. In contrast, states with single-party control over redistricting produced a higher number of safe seats, thereby diminishing overall electoral competition.

Primary elections further reinforce polarization by incentivizing candidates to appeal to the most ideologically committed voters. In both parties, primary turnout tends to skew toward individuals with more extreme views, as moderates and independents are less likely to participate in these contests.

Primary elections further reinforce polarization by incentivizing candidates to appeal to the most ideologically committed voters. In both parties, primary turnout tends to skew toward individuals with more extreme views, as moderates and independents are less likely to participate in these contests.

For example, during the 2024 Republican primaries, several high-profile candidates adopted hardline stances on immigration and tax policy to secure their base's support. Similarly, Democratic candidates in progressive districts faced pressure to back policies like Medicare for All or expansive climate legislation, even when such positions might alienate general election voters.

This dynamic often produces nominees who are less representative of the broader electorate, making bipartisan compromise in governance increasingly unlikely. General election voters are then left choosing between two ideologically rigid candidates, further entrenching partisan divisions.

Bipartisanship, once considered a hallmark of effective governance, has been in steep decline over the past several decades. Congressional voting records reveal that members of both parties are increasingly less likely to support legislation proposed by the opposing party, even on issues that previously enjoyed bipartisan consensus.

Consider infrastructure spending, historically a bipartisan priority. In 2021, President Biden's infrastructure bill passed with only 19 Republican votes in the Senate and 13 in the House, despite widespread agreement on the need for investment in roads, bridges, and broadband. The sharp partisan divide over a traditionally nonpartisan issue reflects the extent to which cooperation has eroded.

This decline is fueled by multiple factors, including gerrymandered districts, partisan primaries, and the increasing influence of party leadership in setting legislative agendas. Representatives and senators are often more concerned with maintaining party loyalty than addressing constituent needs, fearing primary challenges or leadership reprisals if they step out of line.

The lack of bipartisanship undermines legislative effectiveness, as gridlock becomes the default outcome. Critical issues like immigration reform, climate policy, and healthcare remain unresolved, leaving the public frustrated and disillusioned with government. Reforms such as restoring earmarks to encourage cross-party dealmaking or implementing ranked-choice voting to incentivize broader coalitions could help restore some degree of bipartisanship.

The judiciary, traditionally seen as an impartial arbiter of justice, has become a significant battleground in the fight over political polarization. Decisions on contentious issues like gun rights, voting access, and healthcare increasingly reflect partisan divides, contributing to public skepticism about the judiciary's neutrality.

Lower courts are also deeply affected by this polarization. The increasing politicization of judicial appointments, especially at the federal level, has fostered a perception that judges align with the ideologies of the parties that appoint them. This perception erodes the judiciary's role as an independent check on legislative and executive powers, further entrenching political divisions.

Restoring trust in the judiciary will require systemic reforms. Measures such as term limits for federal judges, bipartisan commissions for judicial appointments, or changes to how courts handle highly politicized cases could mitigate the perception of partisanship. These steps would not only help rebuild public confidence but also reduce the judiciary's role as a focal point for political conflict.

Polarization has also eroded long-standing institutional norms, enabling gridlock and partisanship to thrive. Filibuster abuse in the Senate is one such example. Originally intended as a tool for minority voices to delay legislation, the filibuster has evolved into a weapon for blocking almost all major legislation.

Another example is the weakening of oversight mechanisms. Congressional investigations, once used to ensure accountability and transparency, are increasingly wielded as partisan tools. This undermines their legitimacy and reduces their effectiveness in addressing genuine governance failures.

The erosion of norms extends beyond legislative bodies. Executive orders have become a preferred method of governance, bypassing Congress entirely. While this allows presidents to enact policies unilaterally, it exacerbates polarization by making significant policy changes vulnerable to reversal with each administration.

Restoring these norms will require a cultural shift within institutions. This includes reestablishing mutual respect among legislators, enforcing accountability mechanisms that transcend partisanship, and limiting the use of tools like the filibuster to their original purposes.

Institutions are not inherently polarizing, but when their structures and norms are manipulated for partisan gain, they become drivers of division. Gerrymandering, primary elections, judicial appointments, and legislative norms all play a role in reinforcing polarization, but they also present opportunities for reform.

Addressing these challenges will require a commitment to systemic change. Independent redistricting commissions, open primaries, ranked-choice voting, judicial term limits, and filibuster reform are just a few of the solutions that could help mitigate institutional polarization. However, implementing these reforms will require bipartisan buy-in and public pressure, as entrenched interests often resist changes that threaten their power.

Institutions shape how we engage with politics and how society manages its differences, making them a central force in polarization. Their influence touches everything from how leaders are elected to how policies are debated and enacted. If these structures are to foster unity instead of division, reform is essential.

The next section, *The Polarization of Power*, delves into how institutional dynamics intertwine with cultural and social divides. These intersections reveal not just how power is wielded but also how it's contested in today's polarized landscape. By examining these forces, we can better understand the challenges facing governance and collective action—and begin to uncover the pathways toward a more cohesive society.

The Polarization of Power

Polarization doesn't just divide individuals—it fundamentally alters how power is wielded and distributed within societies. As political divides deepen, power becomes concentrated, institutions lose credibility, and the ability to address shared challenges is diminished. This section examines the ways in which polarization reshapes governance, leadership, and decision-making, from the national stage to local communities.

Polarized environments create a gravitational pull toward centralized power, where control is consolidated within party leadership or dominant figures. Political parties increasingly demand ideological purity, leaving little room for dissent or diverse perspectives. Representatives are often pressured to toe the party line, even when doing so conflicts with their personal convictions or the needs of their constituents.

A vivid example is party discipline during major legislative votes. Politicians who break ranks to vote against their party risk losing committee assignments, funding for reelection campaigns, or party support altogether. This dynamic reinforces an "us vs. them" mentality, where loyalty to the party outweighs independent decision-making.

In such environments, "strongman" leadership becomes more prevalent. Leaders who project uncompromising authority and ideological purity gain prominence, appealing to polarized electorates who view opposition as an existential threat. While this can create short-term cohesion within a party, it often leads to long-term instability, as centralized power excludes moderates and alienates diverse voices.

The risks are clear: centralized, polarized power fosters division and weakens the ability of governments to respond flexibly to complex challenges. Restoring space for independent thought and bipartisan cooperation is essential to counteract this trend.

As polarization intensifies, trust in institutions—Congress, the presidency, the judiciary, and even law enforcement—diminishes. Institutions that once served as impartial arbiters of policy or justice are increasingly seen as partisan tools, further eroding their credibility.

Congress exemplifies this loss of trust. Legislative bodies are perceived as gridlocked and ineffective, driven more by party loyalty than by problem-solving. Similarly, the judiciary faces growing scrutiny as court decisions align with partisan expectations, fueling perceptions of bias.

The weaponization of institutional power exacerbates this cynicism. When one party gains control of a branch of government, it often uses that power to advance partisan agendas rather than uphold democratic principles. For example, using law enforcement agencies to investigate political opponents or manipulating judicial appointments to ensure favorable rulings deepens public skepticism and undermines the rule of law.

The consequences are severe. Without trust in institutions, checks and balances weaken, and democratic norms erode. Restoring this trust will require depoliticizing institutional functions and reestablishing their role as neutral guarantors of democracy.

Polarized politics frequently results in legislative paralysis, where governments fail to address critical issues. Climate change, healthcare reform, and infrastructure investment are just a few examples of challenges that demand urgent action but remain mired in partisan gridlock.

Take the debate over healthcare reform. Despite widespread agreement that the system needs improvement, efforts to enact meaningful changes often collapse due to partisan divisions. Each side prioritizes defeating the other's proposals over finding common ground, leaving millions of Americans without adequate coverage or affordable care.

This gridlock frustrates the public, driving disengagement and further polarization. When voters see their government failing to act, they lose faith in its ability to solve problems. This disillusionment creates a feedback loop, where frustration with inaction leads to more polarized voting patterns, perpetuating the cycle of gridlock.

Breaking this cycle will require structural reforms, such as reimagining how legislation is crafted or incentivizing bipartisan collaboration through changes in congressional rules. Without such measures, polarization will continue to paralyze governance, leaving critical challenges unaddressed.

National polarization doesn't stop at the federal level—it filters down to state and local governments, reshaping how decisions are made in communities across the country. Even nonpartisan bodies, such as school boards and city councils, are increasingly drawn into ideological battles.

Consider the recent controversies over public education. School boards, once focused on local issues like curriculum standards or budgets, have become battlegrounds over national debates, including critical race theory and LGBTQ+ rights. These disputes often escalate into heated confrontations, undermining the ability of local leaders to focus on practical governance.

Zoning laws and public safety initiatives have also become ideologically charged. Policies that should be straightforward, such as determining where to build affordable housing or how to allocate police funding, are reframed as partisan litmus tests, making collaboration nearly impossible.

Local governance is critical to community well-being, yet polarization threatens its effectiveness. Rebuilding trust at this level requires fostering dialogue and emphasizing shared goals rather than divisive rhetoric. Communities that successfully navigate polarization often do so by prioritizing local solutions over national politics.

In polarized environments, democratic processes themselves can become tools for consolidating power. Tactics like gerrymandering, voter suppression, and misinformation are used to manipulate electoral outcomes and maintain partisan control.

Gerrymandering, where district boundaries are drawn to favor one party, ensures "safe" seats that protect incumbents from competition. This discourages accountability and amplifies polarization by enabling representatives to appeal only to their base. Similarly, voter suppression efforts, such as restricting access to mail-in ballots or imposing stringent ID requirements, disproportionately affect marginalized groups, undermining the inclusivity of democracy.

Misinformation further exacerbates these challenges. False narratives about voter fraud or election integrity erode public trust in the democratic process, leading to disengagement or, worse, violence. The events of January 6, 2021, are a stark reminder of how misinformation can mobilize individuals to challenge the legitimacy of elections, with devastating consequences for democracy.

Reversing these trends requires safeguarding democratic processes. Expanding access to voting, ensuring transparent redistricting, and combating misinformation are vital steps in restoring public confidence in the system.

Polarization reshapes power dynamics in profound ways, influencing governance, leadership, and decision-making at every level. From the consolidation of authority within political parties to the fracturing of local communities, the impacts are far-reaching. Yet within these challenges lies the potential for reform and renewal.

Polarization Beyond Borders

While American political polarization feels distinct, it is far from unique. Across the globe, societies grapple with similar divisions driven by ideology, economics, and cultural identity. From the deep fractures of Brexit in the United Kingdom to the populist surge in Hungary, polarization manifests in different forms, yet shares common drivers and consequences. By examining global parallels, we can better understand America's challenges, while drawing lessons from countries that have navigated polarization to bridge divides.

Political polarization isn't confined to the United States—it is a recurring theme in democracies worldwide. The United Kingdom's Brexit referendum is a prime example. The 2016 vote to leave the European Union created a fault line in British society, dividing families, communities, and political parties. For many, the debate wasn't just about policy; it became a battle over identity, with one side viewing Brexit as reclaiming sovereignty and the other seeing it as isolationism and regression. Years later, the UK remains deeply divided, with trust in government and unity among its citizens severely eroded.

In Brazil, polarization revolves around the stark right-left divide, exemplified by the presidencies of Jair Bolsonaro and Luiz Inácio Lula da Silva. Bolsonaro's conservative nationalism clashed with Lula's progressive agenda, creating an environment where political opponents are seen as existential threats. This dynamic has fueled mass protests, disinformation campaigns, and a widening cultural divide that echoes many aspects of the U.S. political landscape.

Hungary offers another cautionary tale. Under Viktor Orbán's leadership, polarization has shifted from ideological competition to the consolidation of power. Orbán's government has used nationalist rhetoric to stoke division, framing migrants and liberal elites as threats to Hungarian values. This strategy has allowed his party to marginalize opposition and undermine democratic institutions, demonstrating how polarization can erode democracy when left unchecked.

While the specifics of polarization vary, many of its drivers are universal. Economic inequality, for instance, is a common thread. Societies with widening wealth gaps often experience heightened tensions as economic anxiety feeds resentment. In both the U.S. and Brazil, economic struggles have deepened mistrust between different groups, with the working class often feeling overlooked or exploited by elites.

Social media also plays a central role. Platforms like Facebook and Twitter amplify divisive content, creating echo chambers where users are exposed primarily to ideas that reinforce their beliefs. This phenomenon transcends borders, shaping political discourse in countries as diverse as India, Germany, and Kenya. By prioritizing engagement over accuracy, social media platforms exacerbate polarization, spreading misinformation and heightening ideological divides.

Migration is another global driver. In Europe, debates over immigration policies have polarized nations, with right-wing parties gaining traction by framing migrants as economic and cultural threats. Similar narratives have fueled division in the United States, where immigration has become a flashpoint for partisan battles.

While polarization poses significant challenges, some countries have demonstrated pathways to reconciliation. South Africa's Truth and Reconciliation Commission (TRC) is a powerful example. Following decades of apartheid, the TRC provided a platform for victims and perpetrators to share their stories, fostering understanding and healing. Though far from perfect, the process emphasized the importance of dialogue and accountability in bridging divides.

New Zealand offers another model. The country has managed to maintain relatively low levels of political polarization, partly due to its proportional representation electoral system, which encourages coalition-building and cross-party collaboration. By creating a political structure that rewards compromise, New Zealand has avoided many of the entrenched divisions seen in other democracies.

Germany's post-World War II efforts to confront its history of Nazism also provide valuable insights. Through education, public memorials, and strict laws against hate speech, Germany has worked to foster a culture of accountability and inclusion. These measures have helped to mitigate some of the polarizing forces that might otherwise dominate its political landscape.

While polarization is a global phenomenon, the U.S. experience is shaped by distinct historical and cultural factors. America's two-party system, for example, creates a binary framework that inherently simplifies and amplifies divisions. Unlike proportional representation systems, the winner-takes-all approach incentivizes parties to mobilize their most loyal bases, often at the expense of broader coalition-building.

Cultural factors also play a significant role. The United States has long been characterized by its emphasis on individualism and freedom, values that can both unite and divide. These ideals have fostered a deeply competitive political culture, where compromise is often viewed as weakness. Historical legacies, such as racial inequality and regional divides, further complicate the picture, embedding structural challenges that fuel polarization.

Additionally, the U.S. media landscape is uniquely fragmented, with a proliferation of partisan outlets that reinforce ideological silos. While other countries also grapple with media-driven polarization, the scale and influence of American media make it particularly impactful.

The challenges of polarization, though varied in their specifics, share a common thread: the erosion of trust. Whether in the U.S., the UK, or Brazil, polarization thrives on narratives that pit "us" against "them," creating divisions that undermine democratic institutions and societal cohesion. Yet the examples of South

Africa, New Zealand, and Germany show that reconciliation is possible when societies prioritize dialogue, accountability, and structural reform.

For the United States, these global lessons offer both caution and hope. They underscore the importance of addressing root causes—economic inequality, media fragmentation, and social mistrust—while highlighting the potential for innovative approaches to bridge divides. By looking beyond its borders, the U.S. can find inspiration for strategies that foster unity and rebuild trust in its institutions.

As we move forward, it's essential to remember that polarization is *not* inevitable. Say it with me! It is not inevitable. While its specifics may vary, the underlying challenges are universal—and so are the solutions. By learning from global experiences, Americans can begin to envision a future where divisions no longer define their democracy.

Media and Technology

In today's world, media and technology are inseparable forces shaping how we understand each other, our society, and our politics. Once heralded as tools for connection and enlightenment, these platforms have increasingly become engines of division. Media no longer merely reflects public opinion; it molds it, amplifying the divisions and narratives that fuel polarization.

The evolution of media and technology—from a few shared broadcast channels to an infinite array of digital outlets—has transformed not just how we consume information, but how we think and engage with the world around us. These shifts have fragmented our collective understanding of reality, creating echo chambers that reinforce ideological divisions and distrust.

This chapter delves into the interplay between media, technology, and polarization. It explores how changes in media platforms have reshaped political discourse, eroded trust in institutions, and contributed to the widening chasms within society. Through an analysis of historical trends, the mechanics of modern platforms, and their influence on social and political dynamics, we'll uncover the foundational role media plays in today's polarized landscape.

The Evolution of Media and Its Role in Polarization

The media landscape was not always so fractured. In the mid-20th century, broadcast networks like CBS, NBC, and ABC dominated the airwaves, delivering news and entertainment to a shared national audience. These networks operated under the Fairness Doctrine, a policy implemented by the Federal Communications Commission (FCC) in 1949. The doctrine required broadcasters to present balanced perspectives on controversial issues, ensuring that the public received a diversity of viewpoints.

This era of shared media created a common informational framework. Americans, regardless of political affiliation, consumed much of the same news, shaping a national dialogue rooted in a relatively unified understanding of events. Walter Cronkite, often called "the most trusted man in America," was a symbol of this period—a journalist whose reporting was widely seen as impartial and reliable.

However, the repeal of the Fairness Doctrine in 1987 marked the beginning of a seismic shift in media. Without the requirement to present balanced perspectives, news outlets began to pursue niche audiences, tailoring content to align with specific ideologies. This transformation accelerated with the rise of cable television in the 1980s and 1990s. Channels like Fox News, MSNBC, and CNN offered 24-hour news coverage, but their formats often prioritized sensationalism and opinion-driven programming over balanced reporting.

The fragmentation of media intensified further with the advent of the internet and social media in the early 2000s. Platforms like Facebook, YouTube, and Twitter democratized content creation, allowing anyone with an internet connection to share their views with a global audience. While this democratization had its benefits—giving voice to marginalized communities and fostering new forms of activism—it also opened the floodgates to misinformation, conspiracy theories, and hyper-partisan content.

As media fragmented, so too did the ideal of "objective" journalism. In the mid-20th century, journalistic norms emphasized neutrality, with reporters striving to separate fact from opinion. Today, however, many outlets have abandoned this model in favor of more explicitly partisan approaches.

Partisan news channels and digital outlets now dominate the media landscape. Fox News, for example, has built its brand around conservative commentary, while MSNBC caters to liberal audiences. These outlets don't just report the news; they frame it in ways that reinforce their viewers' existing beliefs. This shift has blurred the line between reporting and opinion, leaving audiences with vastly different interpretations of the same events.

Social media has further eroded the concept of objective journalism. Algorithms prioritize content that generates engagement, which often means promoting sensational or emotionally charged stories. This dynamic rewards extreme viewpoints and penalizes nuanced reporting, creating a media environment where outrage is more valuable than accuracy.

The consequences are profound. When news becomes a tool for affirming beliefs rather than challenging them, it undermines the public's ability to engage critically with information. Instead of fostering dialogue, media becomes a battleground for ideological warfare.

Perhaps the most significant consequence of media fragmentation is the loss of a shared informational framework. In the mid-20th century, Americans could disagree on policy but largely agreed on basic facts. Today, however, even reality is contested.

This divergence is evident in public perceptions of major events. Consider the 2020 U.S. presidential election. While multiple investigations confirmed the election's integrity, misinformation campaigns led millions to believe it was stolen49. These narratives were amplified by partisan media outlets and social media platforms, creating parallel realities where citizens couldn't agree on the legitimacy of the results.

The loss of a common framework extends beyond politics. Issues like climate change, public health, and economic policy are often framed in ways that align with ideological agendas, leaving little room for consensus. This polarization of facts makes it nearly impossible to have productive conversations about complex challenges, as individuals base their arguments on entirely different sets of assumptions.

The fragmentation of media also contributes to social isolation. As people gravitate toward ideologically aligned news sources, they become less likely to encounter opposing viewpoints. This phenomenon, known as the "echo chamber effect," reinforces biases and deepens divisions. Research has shown that individuals who consume partisan media are more likely to view members of the opposing party as threats, further entrenching the "us vs. them" mentality.

The evolution of media has set the stage for the polarized environment we see today. The shift from shared broadcast networks to fragmented cable and digital media has reshaped how people consume and interpret information. The decline of objective journalism and the rise of partisan outlets have created a media landscape where facts are often secondary to ideology. And the loss of a common informational framework has made it harder for individuals to find common ground, even on issues of shared concern.

Understanding this evolution is critical to addressing polarization. Media is not just a reflection of societal divides; it is a driver of them. By examining how these changes came to be, we can begin to identify opportunities for reform and innovation. Whether through promoting media literacy, holding platforms accountable, or fostering dialogue across divides, there is potential to rebuild the trust and cohesion that fragmented media has eroded.

The next sections of this chapter will explore these dynamics in greater detail. From the role of algorithms and misinformation to the generational divide in media consumption, we'll uncover the forces that shape today's media landscape—and consider how they might be harnessed to reduce polarization rather than deepen it.

The Algorithmic & AI Divide

The rapid rise of social media has fundamentally transformed how people consume information and interact with the world. What was once celebrated as a tool for connection and democratized communication has become a powerful driver of division. At the heart of this transformation lies the role of algorithms—complex, data-driven systems designed to prioritize user engagement. While these algorithms succeed in keeping people online, they often do so by amplifying divisive, sensational, or emotionally charged content, deepening political and social polarization in the process.

At their core, social media algorithms are designed to keep users on platforms for as long as possible. This goal is driven by the economic model of social media companies, which rely on advertising revenue. The longer users spend scrolling, the more ads they see, and the more profitable the platform becomes.

To achieve this, algorithms analyze vast amounts of user data to determine what content is most likely to capture attention. Posts that evoke strong emotional reactions—whether anger, fear, or excitement—are often prioritized because they drive higher levels of engagement. Research has shown that sensational and divisive content is far more likely to generate clicks, shares, and comments than neutral or balanced information.

This emphasis on engagement creates a dangerous feedback loop. As users interact with content that aligns with their interests or biases, algorithms serve them more of the same, reinforcing their existing beliefs. Over time, this process narrows the range of information users are exposed to, creating digital environments where opposing viewpoints are rarely encountered.

One of the most significant consequences of algorithm-driven content curation is the creation of echo chambers—online environments where users encounter information that aligns with their existing beliefs. However, recent research suggests these spaces are more complex than previously assumed. While echo chambers predominantly reinforce users' views, dissenting perspectives are not entirely absent; instead, they are often contested or dismissed in ways that further entrench existing beliefs.

For instance, a user who frequently engages with politically conservative content may find their feed dominated by similar viewpoints. While liberal perspectives might appear occasionally, they are often engaged with defensively, leading to discrediting or reinterpretation rather than open discussion. This phenomenon applies to various topics, from climate change to public health, where opposing views become fodder for further polarization rather than opportunities for dialogue.

Echo chambers deepen division by amplifying the sense of "us versus them." While users in these spaces are exposed to opposing perspectives, the engagement often takes the form of criticism or discrediting, which reinforces existing biases rather than encouraging dialogue. Instead of fostering understanding, these interactions can magnify hostility, as opposing viewpoints are framed as threats to the group's core beliefs. Studies suggest that this dynamic intensifies mistrust and contributes to polarization, as individuals retreat further into ideologically aligned communities where their beliefs are continually validated and opposing views are systematically challenged or dismissed.

The amplification of divisive content by algorithms has turned social media into a breeding ground for misinformation campaigns. These false narratives often spread faster than factual content, shaping public opinion and behavior in profound ways.

Consider the misinformation surrounding natural disasters, such as the conspiracy theories that emerged after the devastating wildfires in California in 2023. Social media platforms were inundated with baseless claims that the fires were started by "directed energy weapons" as part of a secret government plot. Despite the lack of evidence, these theories gained traction, fueled by dramatic imagery and algorithmic prioritization of sensational content. The spread of such narratives diverted attention from genuine discussions about climate change and the need for effective mitigation strategies, undermining public trust in both government agencies and scientific explanations.

Another example is the misinformation that surrounded the 2024 rise in food prices. Viral posts falsely claimed that farmers were being paid by the government to destroy crops to create artificial scarcity. These posts gained millions of views on platforms like TikTok and Facebook, sparking outrage and protests. In reality, supply chain disruptions and climate-related issues were the primary causes of the price hikes. However, the spread of misinformation led to widespread distrust of both the agricultural industry and policymakers, making it more difficult to implement meaningful solutions.

These campaigns highlight the unique dangers posed by algorithm-driven amplification. Social media platforms, unlike traditional media outlets, prioritize content that generates high engagement rather than accuracy. This creates a system where sensational or emotionally charged misinformation is more likely to go viral than factual, nuanced reporting.

The impact extends beyond individual incidents. Misinformation campaigns exploit societal fears and uncertainties, deepening polarization and undermining trust in institutions. In the case of the wildfire conspiracies, they fueled divisions between rural and urban communities, with each blaming the other for spreading false narratives. Similarly, the food price misinformation pitted consumers against policymakers and farmers, further fragmenting public discourse.

Understanding the mechanisms that allow misinformation to flourish is crucial to addressing its consequences. Algorithms that amplify divisive content are not neutral; they shape how people perceive and respond to the world. Combatting this requires both technological reform, such as improving content moderation and transparency, and societal efforts to promote media literacy and critical thinking. Without these interventions, the cycle of misinformation and mistrust will continue to erode the fabric of society.

Artificial intelligence (AI) is the driving force behind the algorithms that power social media platforms. These AI systems analyze vast amounts of user data—likes, shares, comments, search histories, and more—to predict what content will most effectively keep users engaged. By tailoring feeds to individual preferences, these algorithms create highly personalized online experiences. While this technology has brought innovation and convenience, it has also introduced profound challenges that significantly shape the digital landscape and society as a whole.

One of the most pressing issues with AI-driven algorithms is their lack of transparency. Social media companies guard the specifics of their AI systems closely, often citing proprietary technology as the reason for their secrecy. This opacity creates significant barriers for researchers, policymakers, and even the public to understand how these systems function or what unintended consequences they may have. For instance, it remains unclear exactly why certain types of content—particularly divisive or sensational material—are prioritized over others. Without visibility into these processes, it is challenging to hold platforms accountable for the societal impacts of their AI systems.

This lack of transparency extends to the metrics used to train these algorithms. Most AI models in social media are optimized for engagement—a nebulous term that can encompass anything from time spent on the platform to the frequency of interactions with posts. While engagement may seem like a neutral metric, it is often achieved by amplifying emotionally charged content, which tends to capture users' attention more effectively. Content that provokes strong reactions, such as anger, fear, or outrage, tends to gain traction and dominate feeds. This creates a feedback loop where the most polarizing material is rewarded with increased visibility, further dividing audiences and entrenching ideological silos.

The focus on engagement also underscores a fundamental limitation of these systems: AI is not inherently designed to promote accuracy, truth, or social cohesion. Its primary goal is to maximize user activity, regardless of the societal consequences. This design flaw means that the algorithms are more likely to amplify misinformation, conspiracy theories, and extreme opinions than nuanced or moderate perspectives. While some social media companies have introduced measures to counter misinformation—such as fact-checking partnerships or flagged content—these efforts often fall short. The sheer scale of misinformation, combined with the challenge of distinguishing legitimate debate from harmful falsehoods, makes this an uphill battle.

Furthermore, the reliance on AI to moderate content introduces its own set of challenges. Automated systems are often ill-equipped to understand context, nuance, or cultural sensitivities. For example, AI might struggle to differentiate between satire and harmful propaganda or between legitimate criticism and hate speech. This lack of sophistication can result in both over-censorship, where legitimate content is removed, and under-censorship, where harmful material remains accessible. These missteps erode trust in platforms, with critics on all sides accusing social media companies of bias or ineffectiveness.

The implications of these limitations extend far beyond individual platforms. The prioritization of divisive content contributes to broader societal polarization, as users are exposed to increasingly extreme perspectives that confirm their biases. This dynamic erodes trust in institutions, weakens democratic discourse, and makes it more difficult to find common ground on critical issues. Moreover, the global reach of these platforms means that these effects are not confined to any one country; they are felt worldwide, exacerbating tensions in already divided societies.

Despite these challenges, AI itself is not inherently harmful. The problem lies in how it is currently applied and prioritized within the business models of social media companies. If AI systems were optimized for metrics beyond engagement—such as promoting diverse perspectives, fostering constructive dialogue, or reducing the spread of false information—their impact could be far less divisive. For example, platforms could design algorithms that prioritize content promoting verified information or highlight posts encouraging cross-ideological discussions.

Achieving this vision will require significant changes to both the technology and the culture surrounding its use. Social media companies must embrace greater transparency, allowing independent researchers and policymakers to audit their systems and understand their societal impacts. Regulatory frameworks can also play a role, setting standards for algorithmic accountability and ensuring that AI systems align with broader societal values

Additionally, there is potential for AI itself to become part of the solution. Advances in machine learning could enable the development of algorithms better equipped to detect and downrank harmful or misleading content. Collaborative efforts between platforms, researchers, and governments could create shared datasets and tools to combat misinformation more effectively. However, these efforts will only succeed if there is a collective commitment to prioritizing the public good over short-term profit.

Ultimately, addressing the challenges posed by AI-driven algorithms will require a combination of technological innovation, ethical oversight, and societal engagement. These systems are shaping how billions of people perceive and interact with the world, making it essential to ensure they do so in ways that promote understanding rather than division. While the flaws in current AI models are significant, they are not insurmountable. With deliberate action, we can harness the power of AI to create a more equitable and informed digital landscape.

The Generational Divide in Media Consumption

In the modern media landscape, the way people consume news and information varies widely across generations, reflecting the rapid evolution of technology and communication platforms. These differences in media habits don't just shape individual political perspectives; they create distinct, parallel realities that deepen polarization and complicate cross-generational dialogue. Understanding how generational divides in media consumption have emerged—and how they contribute to broader societal divides—is essential for addressing the root causes of polarization.

For younger generations, particularly Millennials and Generation Z, social media platforms have evolved into their primary sources of news and information. What started as entertainment hubs—platforms like TikTok, Instagram, and

YouTube—now serve as de facto news outlets. With highly personalized feeds curated by algorithms, these platforms prioritize content that's designed to grab attention and keep users engaged, blurring the line between information and entertainment.

This shift has revolutionized how younger audiences interact with news. They no longer actively seek out information through traditional channels like newspapers or television broadcasts. Instead, news finds them, passively woven into their daily scrolls. A 30-second TikTok breaking down a political policy might pop up between viral dance challenges and cooking tutorials. A video on climate change might be nestled among memes and influencer lifestyle updates. For these generations, consuming news is less about making time for it and more about absorbing it as part of their broader digital routines.

But here's where it gets tricky—and if you're reading this as part of those younger generations, let's have a moment of honesty. The way news reaches you might feel seamless and efficient, but it comes with some major pitfalls. Social media platforms, built for speed and engagement, often prioritize brevity over depth. Political policies, global conflicts, and nuanced issues are boiled down to snappy soundbites and eye-catching visuals. It's like trying to summarize an entire novel in a single tweet. Important context and complexity are often lost, leaving room for misunderstandings and oversimplifications.

And here's the kicker: social media isn't like your traditional newspaper. There's no editor-in-chief sitting in the background vetting each piece of content for accuracy and fairness. That funny, emotionally charged video about a hot-button issue? It could just as easily be created by someone who has no clue what they're talking about—or worse, someone deliberately spreading misinformation. This leaves younger audiences particularly vulnerable to sensationalized or biased content.

But don't think I'm pointing fingers at you. This isn't a "blame the youth" argument—it's a systemic issue. Social media platforms, driven by algorithms optimized for engagement, have designed these systems to make every scroll as irresistible as the last. The responsibility doesn't lie solely with the user; it's baked into the architecture of these platforms.

So, pause for a moment. The next time you see a news clip with a flashy headline or a viral TikTok dissecting a political event, ask yourself: Who made this? What's their source? And what might they be leaving out? Because while the delivery of information has never been easier, the challenge of understanding and verifying it has never been harder.

This generation's relationship with news is unprecedented, and it's not inherently bad. The accessibility is remarkable. But with great convenience comes great responsibility—and that's something we'll unpack as we dive deeper into these divides. So, are you ready to rethink how you engage with the digital world? Let's keep going.

In contrast, older generations—particularly Baby Boomers and the Silent Generation—tend to stick with what they know: traditional media outlets like cable news, newspapers, and radio. Networks such as Fox News, CNN, and MSNBC dominate their screens, offering 24-hour coverage filled with long-format commentary and in-depth reporting. To these audiences, it's not just news—it's familiar, reliable, and consistent.

Their preference for these outlets makes perfect sense when you consider the media landscape they grew up with. Long before the digital revolution, newspapers hit the front porch every morning, and families gathered around the evening news broadcast to hear trusted anchors break down the day's events. These were the days when Walter Cronkite was "the most trusted man in America," and a single network could reach millions at once. For many older viewers, these habits are deeply ingrained, and cable news has become an extension of that earlier era—only now, it's available around the clock.

And let's face it, cable news knows its audience. These networks cater to their core demographics with topics that resonate deeply: Social Security, healthcare, the economy, and issues that directly impact retirement and stability. The way they frame these stories is tailored to the interests and anxieties of their viewers.

But here's where things get complicated—and if you're someone who swears by your nightly news program, I'm talking to you for a second. While traditional media might feel like a steady source of information, it's not without its flaws. Many outlets lean heavily into ideological narratives. Conservative viewers are drawn to Fox News, while liberals gravitate toward MSNBC or PBS. And before you know it, you're in an echo chamber—just like the younger generations on social media.

That's right. The echo chamber effect isn't unique to TikTok or Instagram. Cable news networks do it too, albeit in a more polished and professional package. You might hear the same perspectives repeated over and over, reinforcing what you already believe and rarely challenging you to think outside your comfort zone.

So, here's a challenge for you: The next time you settle into your favorite news program, take a moment to think critically about what you're watching. Ask yourself: What's the framing here? Is this the whole story, or is there another angle I'm missing? Better yet, try flipping the channel to see how another network is covering the same story.

The goal isn't to abandon the media you trust—it's to engage with it more thoughtfully. Because while traditional media provides depth and continuity, it can also narrow your worldview if you're not careful. And let's be honest, we could all use a little more perspective these days. So, are you ready to take a closer look at what you're tuning into?

These stark differences in media consumption have led to the creation of parallel realities, where different generations—and often different ideological groups within those generations—are exposed to entirely different narratives about the same events. A single news story can be presented in vastly different ways depending on the platform or outlet, leading to divergent interpretations and understandings.

For example, consider a significant political development like the passage of major legislation. On TikTok, a Gen Z user might encounter a short, engaging video breaking down the bill's implications in a highly visual and simplified format. Meanwhile, a Baby Boomer watching cable news might see a lengthy panel discussion analyzing the bill from multiple angles, but with a clear ideological slant based on the network's perspective. The younger viewer may focus on emotional or activist-driven appeals, while the older viewer may receive a partisan interpretation rooted in traditional political frameworks.

These parallel realities make it difficult to establish a shared understanding of facts, let alone engage in meaningful dialogue across generations. When individuals base their opinions on entirely different sets of information, conversations about politics and society often devolve into arguments over the validity of sources or the accuracy of narratives. This breakdown in communication exacerbates existing divides and fosters mistrust between generations.

Bridging the generational divide in media consumption requires more than simply encouraging dialogue; it demands a commitment to media literacy. Media literacy equips individuals with the skills to critically evaluate the content they encounter, recognize bias and misinformation, and seek out diverse perspectives.

For younger generations, media literacy can help them navigate the challenges of social media platforms. By understanding how algorithms prioritize certain types of content, they can take steps to diversify their feeds and actively seek out reputable sources. Media literacy education can also teach them to verify the credibility of information, reducing their susceptibility to viral misinformation.

For older generations, media literacy offers tools to identify bias in traditional media outlets and to engage with digital platforms more effectively. As cable news networks increasingly cater to partisan audiences, older viewers must learn to question the framing of stories and seek out alternative viewpoints. Additionally, becoming more comfortable with digital media can help bridge the gap between generations, fostering greater understanding of how younger people consume and interact with information.

Media literacy programs in schools, libraries, and community organizations can play a vital role in addressing these challenges. By providing intergenerational workshops and resources, these initiatives can create opportunities for individuals of all ages to learn together, share experiences, and develop a more nuanced understanding of the media landscape.

consumption requires more than individual efforts—it demands intentional spaces for cross-generational dialogue and collaboration. And as your trusted, ageless narrator, I'm here to guide you through this endeavor with a mix of timeless wisdom and just enough humor to keep things interesting.

The key lies in creating opportunities for younger and older generations to come together, exchange perspectives, and learn from one another. Imagine community forums where Baby Boomers share their deep historical insights, while Gen Z participants introduce innovative ways to engage with current issues. Mentorship programs and intergenerational advocacy groups could become the foundation for these interactions, fostering understanding while addressing shared challenges like misinformation and polarization. It's not about convincing anyone that their way of consuming media is better—it's about building bridges between the TikTok generation and the nightly news loyalists.

Technology companies, too, must rise to the occasion. Social media platforms and traditional media outlets alike hold immense power in shaping how we interact with information and each other. It's time they prioritize features that promote cross-generational dialogue and highlight diverse perspectives. Imagine algorithms that nudge users toward stories resonating across age groups or platforms spotlighting conversations where Millennials and the Silent Generation find unexpected common ground. These tools wouldn't just reduce the divide; they'd elevate the richness of collective discourse.

This is about more than just fixing a problem—it's about transforming what could be a weakness into a strength. When generations engage in meaningful dialogue, they bring complementary skills and experiences to the table. Younger generations offer a fresh, digital-first perspective on issues, while older generations provide depth, context, and historical memory. Together, they can create solutions that neither could achieve alone.

And as your ever-neutral, always-present narrator, I'll be here, observing this intergenerational collaboration with a mix of optimism and gentle prodding. Because in the end, bridging this divide isn't just about addressing polarization—it's about creating a world where we all learn from one another, respecting the unique insights each generation brings to the conversation.

As technology continues to evolve, the generational divide in media consumption is likely to persist, if not widen. New platforms will emerge, catering to younger audiences with innovative formats, while older generations may continue to rely on more familiar outlets. However, this divide does not have to be a source of conflict.

By prioritizing media literacy, encouraging dialogue, and fostering intergenerational collaboration, society can transform these differences into opportunities for growth and understanding. The key is to recognize that while media consumption habits may differ, the shared goal of staying informed and engaged transcends generational boundaries.

Ultimately, addressing the generational divide in media consumption is not just about bridging gaps in how people access information; it's about fostering a culture that values diverse perspectives, critical thinking, and mutual respect. By doing so, we can build a more informed and united society, capable of navigating the complexities of the modern media landscape.

Solutions for a Polarized Media Landscape

The polarization fueled by media and technology is not inevitable. While these forces have exacerbated divisions, they also hold the potential to foster unity and understanding. By implementing thoughtful strategies and encouraging systemic reforms, we can reshape the media landscape into a tool for bridging divides rather than deepening them. This section explores actionable solutions to mitigate polarization, from empowering individuals with media literacy to reforming the platforms and systems that shape our informational environment.

One of the most effective ways to counteract polarization is by empowering individuals to critically evaluate the information they consume. Media literacy equips people with the skills to identify bias, verify sources, and recognize the tactics used to manipulate emotions and beliefs. In a world where misinformation spreads rapidly, the ability to navigate the media landscape critically is more important than ever.

Media literacy should start early. Schools can play a vital role by integrating media literacy into their curricula, teaching students how to analyze news, understand algorithms, and discern credible sources from unreliable ones. For example, programs like News Literacy Project in the United States provide resources to help young people become more informed media consumers.

For adults, workshops, community programs, and online resources can offer opportunities to improve media literacy. Public libraries, civic organizations, and even employers can organize events or provide materials that teach people how to question what they see online critically. These initiatives not only reduce individual susceptibility to misinformation but also foster a more informed electorate.

The algorithms that drive social media platforms are central to the problem of polarization. These systems, designed to maximize engagement, often prioritize sensational or divisive content, creating echo chambers and amplifying misinformation. To address this, social media companies must embrace greater transparency and accountability.

Regulators and independent researchers should have access to data that reveals how algorithms function, what content they prioritize, and how those decisions affect user behavior. By opening their systems to scrutiny, platforms can build trust and allow for informed discussions about their impact on society.

Platforms can also implement changes to their algorithms that prioritize accuracy and diversity over engagement metrics. For instance, features that highlight content from diverse perspectives or flag potentially misleading posts could help users navigate their feeds more critically. Some platforms, like Twitter and Facebook, have already experimented with these tools, such as labeling misinformation or showing users opposing viewpoints. While these efforts are imperfect, they demonstrate the potential for technology to reduce polarization when used responsibly.

Additionally, the decline of independent journalism has left a gap in the media landscape that partisan outlets and misinformation have rushed to fill. Supporting independent, fact-based journalism is critical to restoring trust and providing balanced perspectives on complex issues.

Public funding for journalism, grants for investigative reporting, and non-profit news organizations are all avenues to strengthen independent media. Initiatives like ProPublica in the United States or The Bureau of Investigative Journalism in the UK demonstrate how independent outlets can produce high-quality, impactful reporting that holds power to account without catering to ideological audiences.

Consumers also have a role to play. Subscribing to reputable news outlets, sharing well-researched articles, and supporting non-profit journalism can help ensure that quality reporting thrives in a media environment dominated by clickbait and partisanship.

The challenges of a polarized media landscape are daunting, but they are not insurmountable. Around the world, countries have implemented strategies that provide valuable lessons in reducing polarization and fostering unity. By examining these initiatives, we can identify practical solutions that address the root causes of media-driven division and help create a more informed and cohesive society.

New Zealand's public media system offers a compelling example of how independent journalism can counter polarization. Outlets like Radio New Zealand, funded by the public and dedicated to balanced reporting, focus on the public interest rather than profit-driven content. This commitment to unbiased journalism has helped create a shared informational framework, allowing citizens to engage with news that emphasizes understanding over division. By prioritizing accuracy and inclusivity, New Zealand's media model demonstrates the potential for public-funded outlets to bridge societal divides.

Finland, on the other hand, has taken a proactive approach to combating misinformation through media literacy education. Starting in elementary school, students are taught to critically evaluate news, identify propaganda, and assess the credibility of digital content. This early intervention equips individuals with the tools needed to navigate an increasingly complex media environment. The result is not only a reduced spread of misinformation but also a society with greater trust in its institutions and media. Finland's emphasis on media literacy highlights the importance of empowering individuals to think critically about the information they consume.

Germany provides another case study in addressing the challenges of the digital age, particularly with its Network Enforcement Act (NetzDG). This legislation requires social media platforms to remove illegal content, such as hate speech or incitement to violence, within 24 hours. While the law has sparked debate about its implications for free speech, it has prompted platforms to take a more active role in content moderation, reducing the prevalence of harmful material online. Germany's approach underscores the potential for regulatory frameworks to hold platforms accountable while mitigating the divisive effects of digital media.

These examples illustrate that change is possible. Whether through robust public media systems, education initiatives, or targeted legislation, each of these countries offers a unique perspective on how to address polarization. Their successes demonstrate that with thoughtful interventions, the media landscape can evolve to support unity rather than division. As we consider these models, it's clear that global collaboration and the sharing of best practices will be essential in tackling the challenges posed by a fragmented and polarized media environment.

The media landscape, as it stands, is both a mirror and a driver of our divisions. Social media algorithms amplify our biases, partisan outlets reinforce our silos, and misinformation thrives in the absence of critical scrutiny. Yet, these challenges also present an opportunity—a chance to rethink how we consume, share, and engage with information.

Throughout this chapter, we've explored the complexities of media and technology's role in polarization, from their generational divides to the impact of algorithms. We've seen how these forces shape not only our individual perspectives but also our collective realities.

The solutions outlined here—promoting media literacy, fostering transparency, supporting independent journalism, and learning from global efforts—are not just strategies to reduce polarization. They are steps toward reclaiming the potential of media and technology as tools for connection, understanding, and progress.

Ultimately, the power to shape a less polarized future lies in our hands. By embracing these changes and demanding better from our media systems, we can begin to bridge the divides that have fractured our society. It's not an easy path, but it's a necessary one—because the stories we tell, the platforms we use, and the perspectives we share will determine the kind of world we create. And isn't that a story worth writing together?

Economic Inequality

Economic inequality, at its core, refers to the uneven distribution of wealth, income, and access to resources within a society. It is a phenomenon that has persisted throughout history, but its scope and impact in modern America are particularly striking. As the wealthiest individuals amass unprecedented fortunes, millions of Americans struggle to meet their basic needs, leaving a growing gap that defines both personal realities and societal dynamics. Understanding economic inequality is crucial not only for addressing poverty but also for tackling its broader implications on democracy, social cohesion, and opportunity.

At first glance, economic inequality might seem like an abstract concept, but its manifestations are deeply personal. It shows up in the paycheck disparities between a CEO and a minimum-wage worker, the resources available in affluent versus underfunded school districts, and the stark contrast in healthcare access between the wealthy and the poor. Wealth inequality, one dimension of this broader issue, is particularly stark. In the United States, the top 1% of wealth holders control about 31% of the nation's total wealth, leaving the remaining 99% to divide what's left. Within that 99%, the bottom 90% holds approximately 69%, meaning the vast majority of Americans share a smaller portion of the pie compared to the wealthiest few.

This discrepancy is more than just a statistical imbalance; it reflects a concentration of economic power that has profound social and political implications. When such a small group wields an outsized share of resources, they have greater influence over policies, markets, and even cultural norms. Meanwhile, the vast majority are left to navigate systemic barriers—underfunded schools, unaffordable healthcare, and stagnant wages—that make economic mobility increasingly unattainable. This disparity creates a society where opportunities are unequally distributed, leaving many to feel disenfranchised and disconnected from the economic progress touted by the wealthy elite. The scale of this imbalance isn't just unfair—it undermines the social cohesion and trust necessary for a functional democracy.

Income inequality, another facet, highlights the disparity in earnings between individuals and groups. The gender pay gap, racial wage disparities, and regional income differences all reflect the structural issues driving unequal earnings. Meanwhile, resource inequality—seen in access to housing, education, and healthcare—further entrenches economic divides. For many Americans, these inequities create a cycle where opportunity is limited not by talent or ambition, but by the circumstances of birth.

Economic inequality doesn't arise in a vacuum. It is the result of systemic factors that have evolved over decades, often exacerbated by policy decisions and global trends. Globalization, for instance, has reshaped economies worldwide, creating opportunities but also new divides. While it has led to cheaper goods and expanded markets, globalization has also resulted in the outsourcing of manufacturing jobs, leaving many American workers—particularly in rural and post-industrial regions—without stable employment opportunities.

Automation has further transformed the economic landscape. As industries adopt advanced technologies to increase efficiency, jobs once performed by humans are increasingly handled by machines. While automation has boosted productivity, it has disproportionately impacted low- and middle-skill jobs, leaving many workers behind. Factory closures, reduced job opportunities, and stagnant wages are the human costs of this technological progress, and they affect diverse communities across the country.

Policy decisions are a key driver of economic inequality, shaping the landscape of opportunities and barriers that determine who thrives and who struggles. Over time, policies that favor the wealthy and large corporations have deepened the economic divide, while reductions in social safety nets have left vulnerable populations without the support they need to succeed. Tax cuts disproportionately benefiting the top earners have exacerbated wealth concentration, allowing the richest Americans to accumulate more power and influence while public resources that could aid low- and middle-income families remain underfunded.

One of the most significant consequences of these policy choices is the erosion of labor protections. The decline of union membership in the United States has drastically weakened the collective bargaining power of workers. Unions historically played a vital role in securing fair wages, reasonable working hours, and essential benefits like healthcare and pensions. However, as union membership has dwindled—falling from over 20% of the workforce in the 1980s to around 10% today—workers have seen their negotiating power diminish. This decline has directly contributed to wage stagnation, even as productivity and corporate profits have soared. Workers, once the backbone of America's middle class, now face precarious employment conditions with limited prospects for economic advancement.

Historical policy decisions have also institutionalized inequality across racial and geographic lines. Take redlining, for example. This discriminatory practice, implemented through federal housing policies in the 20th century, systematically excluded Black Americans from accessing home loans and affordable housing in desirable neighborhoods. By denying Black families the opportunity to build wealth through homeownership—one of the primary vehicles for economic mobility—redlining entrenched generational disparities in wealth and opportunity. Even though redlining was outlawed decades ago, its legacy persists in the form of segregated neighborhoods, underfunded schools, and stark racial wealth gaps.

On the other hand, rural disinvestment has disproportionately affected poor White communities, leaving them grappling with a different set of systemic challenges. Policies that prioritized urban and suburban development often neglected rural areas, resulting in failing infrastructure, underfunded schools, and limited access to healthcare. Manufacturing jobs that once sustained these communities were outsourced or automated, and without significant reinvestment, rural economies have struggled to recover as seen in the income gap. For many, the loss of stable employment opportunities has led to cycles of poverty, declining local economies, and outmigration of young people seeking better prospects elsewhere.

The stark contrast between urban and rural policy impacts underscores how systemic inequality transcends racial and geographic lines. While Black Americans have faced exclusion through practices like redlining, rural White Americans have been sidelined by a lack of investment in their communities. These experiences, though shaped by different policies and historical contexts, reveal a shared reality: both groups have been systematically denied the resources and opportunities necessary to achieve economic stability.

Addressing these entrenched inequalities requires more than acknowledging past mistakes—it demands proactive policy changes that prioritize equity and inclusion. Strengthening labor protections, investing in underserved communities, and creating policies that expand access to education, healthcare, and housing are essential steps. Without such measures, the systemic divides perpetuated by decades of policy decisions will continue to hinder economic mobility and deepen polarization. By understanding how policy has created and perpetuated inequality, we can begin to craft solutions that bridge divides and foster a more equitable society.

It is easy to fall into the trap of viewing economic inequality through the lens of race or political ideology, but the reality is more complex. Poor Americans across racial and ethnic lines often face similar struggles, even if their experiences are shaped by different historical and cultural contexts. Recognizing these shared challenges is essential for building solidarity and addressing inequality as a unifying issue.

Take housing insecurity as an example. For Black Americans, the legacy of discriminatory practices like redlining continues to limit access to affordable housing and perpetuate wealth gaps. Meanwhile, rural White communities also grapple with housing challenges, as a lack of investment and economic opportunity leaves many families in substandard living conditions. While the causes of these struggles differ, the outcomes—a lack of safe, stable housing—are strikingly similar.

Healthcare disparities also cut across racial and geographic lines. Poor Black Americans in urban centers often struggle to access quality care due to systemic racism and underfunded healthcare infrastructure. At the same time, poor White Americans in rural areas face a healthcare crisis driven by hospital closures and provider shortages. Both groups suffer from high rates of chronic illness and limited access to preventive care, reflecting how economic inequality creates shared vulnerabilities.

Even in education, where systemic racism undeniably impacts outcomes for Black and Hispanic students, underfunded rural schools serving predominantly White populations face many of the same challenges. Poor infrastructure, outdated resources, and underpaid teachers are common struggles, whether the school is in an urban neighborhood or a rural town. These parallels highlight that while the contexts may vary, the impacts of economic inequality are deeply felt across diverse communities.

In the face of these shared struggles, economic inequality has the potential to be a unifying issue, transcending cultural and ideological divides. While differences in race, geography, and political affiliation are often emphasized, focusing on common challenges reveals the potential for collaboration. Poor White and Black Americans, for instance, may seem divided along racial lines, but they face many of the same barriers: stagnant wages, limited access to quality education, and declining economic mobility.

This shared reality is often overshadowed by narratives that emphasize division, but addressing inequality requires looking beyond those divides. Policies that increase access to healthcare, improve public education, and invest in affordable housing benefit all low-income communities, regardless of race or location. Similarly, systemic reforms like raising the minimum wage or strengthening labor protections address the needs of diverse groups, creating opportunities for cross-cultural solidarity.

The potential for unity is particularly evident in grassroots movements and community organizations. Across the country, coalitions are forming to tackle issues like housing affordability, healthcare access, and worker rights. These efforts often bring together people from different backgrounds, highlighting the shared interest in addressing economic inequality. By focusing on these commonalities, we can build a more inclusive movement that prioritizes solutions over division.

Economic inequality doesn't just harm individuals—it affects society as a whole. Communities with high levels of inequality experience lower levels of trust, higher rates of crime, and reduced social mobility. Politically, inequality undermines democracy, as the wealthy exert disproportionate influence over policy decisions, leaving marginalized groups with little power to advocate for change. Addressing inequality is not just a moral imperative; it is essential for creating a stable, cohesive society.

The stakes are high, but the opportunities for progress are real. By framing economic inequality as a unifying issue, we can begin to shift the narrative away from division and toward collaboration. Recognizing that poor White Americans and Black Americans share more in common economically than they differ culturally is a crucial step in building solidarity and addressing the systemic factors driving inequality.

Economic inequality is one of the defining challenges of our time, shaping the lives of millions and influencing the trajectory of society. While its manifestations vary across racial, geographic, and cultural lines, its impacts are deeply interconnected. By understanding the systemic factors driving inequality and recognizing the shared struggles faced by diverse groups, we can begin to address this issue not as a point of division, but as a source of unity.

This chapter serves as an invitation to see economic inequality for what it is: a challenge that transcends identity and ideology, demanding collective action and systemic change. By focusing on the commonalities that unite us, rather than the divisions that separate us, we can move toward a future where opportunity and prosperity are accessible to all. The next sections will delve deeper into the specific ways economic inequality shapes lives and explore solutions to bridge the gap. Together, we can build a more equitable society—one where the promise of opportunity is not limited to the fortunate few but extended to all.

How Economic Inequality Shapes Opportunity

Economic inequality is not just about income disparities or wealth gaps; it manifests in everyday life, shaping the opportunities people have to succeed and thrive. The effects ripple through education, healthcare, housing, and career prospects, creating cycles of poverty that are difficult to break. These systemic barriers don't discriminate solely by race or geography—they affect poor communities of all backgrounds, forging a shared experience of hardship. This section delves into the tangible ways economic inequality limits opportunity and perpetuates disadvantage.

Education is often heralded as the great equalizer, but economic inequality has turned it into a system that perpetuates disparities. In low-income areas, whether predominantly White, Black, or Hispanic, schools are often underfunded and under-resourced. Funding for public schools in the United States is heavily reliant on local property taxes, meaning that wealthier neighborhoods can afford better schools, while poorer communities are left with fewer resources.

The consequences are stark. Students in underfunded schools often face overcrowded classrooms, outdated textbooks, and limited access to extracurricular activities or advanced placement courses. For example, a school in an affluent suburb might offer state-of-the-art science labs and multiple foreign language options, while a school in a low-income rural or urban area may struggle to provide even basic supplies. This disparity reinforces inequality, as children from wealthier families are better prepared for higher education and lucrative careers, while their peers in low-income areas are left at a disadvantage.

The effects of these inequities are evident in graduation rates and college admissions. Students from low-income families are less likely to attend college, and those who do often carry the burden of substantial debt, further limiting their economic mobility. These barriers compound over time, ensuring that economic inequality is passed from one generation to the next.

Access to healthcare is another critical area where economic inequality shapes opportunity. Poor Americans of all backgrounds face significant challenges in obtaining affordable and quality medical care. Whether in urban neighborhoods or rural towns, economic barriers often determine who receives preventive care, who manages chronic conditions effectively, and who faces catastrophic medical bills.

For low-income Black Americans, systemic racism has compounded the challenges of healthcare access. Many predominantly Black neighborhoods lack adequate healthcare facilities, forcing residents to travel long distances for basic services. Rural White Americans face a different but equally daunting challenge: the closure of rural hospitals and clinics, which has created healthcare deserts in many parts of the country.

The lack of preventive care is particularly troubling. Poor Americans are more likely to suffer from chronic illnesses like diabetes, heart disease, and hypertension, yet they are less likely to receive regular checkups or early interventions. This results in higher healthcare costs over time and worse health outcomes, perpetuating a cycle where economic hardship and poor health reinforce one another.

Housing stands at the intersection of economic inequality and opportunity, revealing stark disparities shaped by race, geography, and systemic neglect. For Black Americans, the historical exclusion from homeownership through practices like redlining has left a legacy of economic disadvantage. Although formally outlawed decades ago, redlining's impact endures: Black families remain less likely to own homes, a critical means of building generational wealth, and are often concentrated in neighborhoods with underfunded schools, limited job opportunities, and higher crime rates. This isn't just a relic of the past—it's an ongoing barrier to economic mobility and stability.

In rural areas, poor White Americans face a different but equally pervasive housing crisis. Decades of disinvestment have left many rural communities without the infrastructure necessary to support affordable housing markets. As stable industries like manufacturing and mining have vanished, so too have the opportunities that once allowed these families to maintain a foothold in the middle class. Many now contend with substandard housing, rising rates of homelessness, and an economic stagnation that leaves little room for progress.

What unites these communities—urban and rural, Black and White—is the disproportionate burden housing costs place on low-income families. Across the board, those with the least resources often spend the greatest percentage of their income on housing, leaving little for other necessities like healthcare, education, or savings. These financial strains perpetuate cycles of poverty, making upward mobility an elusive goal.

Breaking these cycles requires more than addressing housing costs; it demands targeted reinvestment in both urban and rural communities. Expanding affordable housing initiatives, improving access to economic opportunities, and fostering equitable urban planning are steps that can make homeownership and stable living conditions attainable for all. The housing crisis is not just about buildings and mortgages—it's about restoring pathways to opportunity and ensuring that no community, urban or rural, is left behind.

Economic inequality also shapes career opportunities, with profound implications for upward mobility. Workers in low-wage jobs, often in retail, food service, or gig economy roles, face limited prospects for advancement. These jobs often lack benefits like healthcare, paid leave, or retirement plans, making it difficult for workers to achieve financial stability.

The decline of union membership has further weakened workers' bargaining power, leading to wage stagnation and poor working conditions. This is particularly true for low- and middle-skill jobs, which have been disproportionately affected by globalization and automation. As factories close and jobs are outsourced, workers in rural areas and post-industrial towns are left with few alternatives. Meanwhile, urban workers in similar economic brackets face stiff competition for low-paying service jobs, creating a parallel struggle in different geographic contexts.

For many poor Americans, the dream of upward mobility remains elusive. Systemic barriers, such as the rising cost of higher education and the decline of vocational training programs, further limit their ability to access higher-paying careers. This lack of opportunity traps individuals and families in cycles of poverty, reinforcing the broader trends of economic inequality.

Economic inequality isn't just an issue of individual hardship; it disrupts the very fabric of society. When basic opportunities like education, healthcare, housing, and stable careers are dictated by economic status rather than merit or effort, the foundational promise of the American Dream becomes unattainable for millions. This pervasive inequality creates a system where upward mobility is not only limited but often impossible, perpetuating cycles of poverty and division.

Addressing these disparities demands systemic change. Investing in public education can ensure that every child, regardless of their zip code, has access to quality schools and the tools to succeed. Expanding affordable housing initiatives can provide stability to families who might otherwise face homelessness or unsafe living conditions. Ensuring universal access to healthcare would prevent financial ruin caused by illness while promoting overall societal well-being. At the same time, policies that strengthen worker protections—such as raising the minimum wage, ensuring paid leave, and revitalizing union representation—can create pathways to financial security and stability for those in low-income jobs.

These challenges, while significant, are not insurmountable. Recognizing the shared struggles of diverse communities is key to fostering collective action and designing inclusive solutions. By addressing the structural barriers that perpetuate inequality, we can begin to rebuild a society where opportunity is not a luxury afforded to the few but a fundamental right available to all. The pursuit of equity benefits everyone by creating a stronger, more cohesive, and more just society.

Wealth and Power—A Growing Divide

Economic inequality in the United States is about more than income gaps or the accumulation of wealth—it's about the disproportionate power that comes with extreme wealth concentration. As the wealthiest Americans amass fortunes and wield influence that shapes policy and politics, the gap between the elite and the rest grows wider. Meanwhile, low- and middle-income Americans struggle with stagnant wages, rising costs, and diminishing opportunities. This divide creates a pervasive "rich vs. the rest" dynamic that impacts every facet of society, fostering shared grievances among the working poor across racial and cultural lines.

In the United States, wealth has always been closely linked to power, but the sway of the wealthiest individuals and corporations has grown to unprecedented levels. By channeling billions of dollars into political campaigns, lobbying, and funding research institutions, the elite have shaped policies to prioritize their interests over those of the broader population. From tax incentives to relaxed regulations, the agenda of the wealthy often dominates, leaving the needs of low- and middle-income Americans sidelined.

Consider the pharmaceutical industry as an example. Large pharmaceutical companies have used their immense financial resources to influence drug pricing policies, ensuring they maintain high profit margins. Despite widespread public outcry over exorbitant prescription drug costs, meaningful reform has been slow to materialize. Lobbying by pharmaceutical companies, which spend hundreds of millions annually to sway lawmakers, has stymied efforts to introduce measures like price caps or negotiate drug prices through Medicare. As a result, many Americans—especially those in low-income households—struggle to afford essential medications, while the industry's profits soar.

The influence of wealth also shapes the broader policy agenda, often prioritizing the preservation of elite assets over addressing urgent public concerns. Key issues like comprehensive climate action, affordable housing, and equitable education funding are frequently deprioritized in favor of policies that benefit the affluent, such as subsidies for industries like fossil fuels or real estate. This dynamic creates a sense of disenfranchisement among many Americans, who see their needs consistently overshadowed by corporate interests.

As these patterns persist, trust in institutions continues to erode. For millions of Americans, the government increasingly appears to function as a tool of the wealthy rather than a champion of the public good. This perception undermines social cohesion, leaving many to question whether a system so deeply influenced by wealth can ever truly serve the collective interests of society.

The concentration of wealth has also exacerbated societal divisions, fostering a "rich vs. the rest" dynamic that fuels resentment and inequality. For the wealthiest Americans, opportunities abound. They live in affluent neighborhoods with the best schools, access premium healthcare, and benefit from investment opportunities that generate even more wealth. In contrast, low- and middle-income families face rising housing costs, unaffordable childcare, and limited access to education or healthcare. These struggles are not just economic—they shape every aspect of life, from physical and mental health to the ability to plan for the future.

This divide is particularly visible in moments of crisis. During the COVID-19 pandemic, for instance, billionaires saw their collective wealth increase by trillions of dollars, while millions of

Americans faced job losses, eviction, and food insecurity. Such disparities reinforce the perception that the system is rigged in favor of the elite, fueling frustration and a sense of injustice among those left behind.

While wealth inequality creates a stark divide between the rich and the rest, it also highlights the shared struggles of poor and working-class Americans across racial and cultural lines. Wage stagnation is a key issue that unites these groups. Despite increases in worker productivity over the past few decades, wages for low- and middle-income workers have remained largely stagnant when adjusted for inflation. This has left many families struggling to cover basic expenses like rent, groceries, and healthcare.

The lack of affordable childcare is another shared grievance. Whether in urban neighborhoods predominantly home to Black and Hispanic families or rural areas with large White populations, the high cost of childcare places a significant burden on working parents. Without access to affordable options, many parents are forced to leave the workforce or rely on informal, often unreliable care arrangements. This not only limits their earning potential but also perpetuates economic instability.

Housing is yet another point of convergence. Low-income Americans, regardless of race or geography, are more likely to spend a disproportionate share of their income on housing, leaving little room for other necessities. Poor Black Americans in urban areas often face housing shortages and gentrification, while poor White Americans in rural areas contend with substandard housing and disinvestment. Both groups experience the destabilizing effects of insecure housing, underscoring the shared challenges of economic inequality.

One of the most significant barriers to addressing economic inequality is the tendency to frame it through the lens of identity politics. Racial and cultural divisions are often emphasized in public discourse, distracting from the structural factors that perpetuate inequality. This focus on division benefits the wealthy elite, as it prevents marginalized groups from uniting around shared economic interests.

Reframing economic inequality as a common challenge rather than a divisive issue is essential for fostering collective action. Poor White Americans and Black Americans, for instance, may face different historical and cultural contexts, but their struggles with stagnant wages, unaffordable childcare, and housing insecurity reveal a shared reality. Recognizing these commonalities is the first step toward building alliances that can advocate for systemic change.

Grassroots movements and community organizations provide examples of how this unity can be achieved. Groups focused on workers' rights, affordable housing, or healthcare access often bring together people from diverse backgrounds, demonstrating that shared economic struggles can transcend racial or cultural differences. By shifting the focus from what divides us to what unites us, these efforts lay the groundwork for a more inclusive and equitable future.

The growing divide between the wealthy elite and the rest of society is one of the most pressing challenges of our time. It is a divide that shapes not only economic outcomes but also political power, social cohesion, and the prospects for future generations. As the wealthiest Americans wield disproportionate influence, the voices and needs of low- and middle-income families—regardless of race or geography—are often sidelined.

Addressing this divide requires systemic changes that redistribute power and resources more equitably. Policies that strengthen labor protections, invest in affordable housing and childcare, and ensure access to quality healthcare and education can help level the playing field. Equally important is the need to reframe economic inequality as a unifying issue, emphasizing the shared struggles of the working poor over the divisions that have long been exploited to maintain the status quo.

By recognizing the commonalities between diverse groups and working together to address structural inequities, we can begin to bridge the growing divide and create a society where opportunity and prosperity are not the privileges of the few but the rights of all. This isn't just an economic imperative—it's a moral one, and it demands action from every corner of society.

The End Solution

Economic inequality does not exist in a vacuum—it is shaped and perpetuated by the systems we build and the priorities we set as a society. At its core, the structure of modern capitalism ties fundamental human needs, such as healthcare and housing, to one's ability to generate income. For millions of Americans, this system creates an inescapable cycle where the right to live with dignity and security depends on their capacity to sell their labor. To break this cycle and foster a more equitable society, we must move beyond a purely capitalist framework and embrace a mix of systems that prioritize both economic growth and the well-being of all citizens.

Healthcare in the United States is a stark example of what happens when essential services are left to market forces. Unlike in many other developed nations, access to healthcare in the U.S. is primarily tied to employment. This system leaves millions of Americans without coverage when they lose their jobs or are unable to work due to illness, disability, or caregiving responsibilities. Even for those who are insured, the cost of medical care can be crippling, with high deductibles, co-pays, and out-of-pocket expenses driving many into debt.

This creates a paradox where individuals must remain healthy to work but need to work to afford healthcare. For low-income Americans, this often means delaying or foregoing medical treatment, exacerbating health disparities and reinforcing cycles of poverty. When citizens are forced to choose between basic survival and their physical well-being, it's clear the system is failing.

Housing, another fundamental human need, faces similar challenges under a market-driven system. Rising rent costs and housing shortages have left millions unable to afford stable living conditions. For the working poor, the dream of homeownership—a key driver of wealth accumulation—remains out of reach. Market forces alone cannot address these crises; systemic intervention is necessary to ensure equitable access to these essential resources.

To address these challenges, a hybrid approach that incorporates elements of socialism and capitalism is needed. Such a system would preserve the innovation and efficiency associated with market-driven economies while ensuring that basic needs are guaranteed for all citizens. This is not a radical idea—it's a practical solution that many countries already implement.

Universal healthcare is one example of how a mixed system can work. Nations like Canada, the UK, and Germany provide healthcare as a right, funded through taxes and managed by the government or regulated private entities. These systems ensure that no one is left without access to care, regardless of their employment status or income level. By removing profit motives from essential healthcare services, these countries have achieved better health outcomes at a lower cost compared to the U.S.

Affordable housing initiatives offer a practical pathway for addressing housing insecurity while accommodating a range of needs and market dynamics. A balanced approach could include the government providing basic, low-cost housing options that, while modest, meet essential living standards and ensure no one is left without shelter. These units would be affordable and accessible, providing a safety net for those who need immediate housing solutions. At the same time, the private market could be incentivized to develop higher-quality housing options for low- and middle-income families, striking a balance between affordability and livability.

This dual-system approach leverages the efficiency and innovation of the private sector while maintaining public sector oversight to ensure equitable access. Government subsidies, rent controls, and zoning reforms could encourage private developers to build affordable units without sacrificing quality. By creating a competitive yet regulated market, this system ensures that everyone, from the most vulnerable to those seeking better housing options, has access to a safe and stable home. Such an approach would reduce homelessness, alleviate housing insecurity, and foster a more inclusive housing market that accommodates diverse needs and aspirations.

Progressive tax reforms are a cornerstone of funding the investments needed to address systemic economic inequality and ensure equitable opportunities for all. In the richest country in the world, the idea that basic necessities like healthcare, education, and housing remain inaccessible to millions while national debt continues to grow is unacceptable. A comprehensive reform of the tax system must not only target the wealthiest individuals and corporations but also involve a fair contribution from all citizens to reflect the collective responsibility of building a thriving and sustainable society.

Taxing the wealthiest individuals and corporations at higher rates is a logical starting point. Over the past few decades, the wealthiest Americans and large corporations have benefited disproportionately from tax cuts and loopholes, allowing them to accumulate unprecedented levels of wealth while contributing relatively less to the public coffers. Restoring and expanding progressive taxation—such as higher income tax brackets for multimillionaires, estate taxes on inheritances over a certain threshold, and closing loopholes that allow corporations to offshore profits—can generate significant revenue. This funding can be directly funneled into transformative programs like universal healthcare, public education, and affordable housing initiatives, creating a foundation for greater equality and mobility.

However, true reform must extend beyond targeting the ultra-rich. Everyone has a role to play in building a better society. A fair tax system that requires modest contributions from middle- and lower-income earners—balanced by tax credits and exemptions to ensure affordability—creates a sense of shared responsibility. For instance, small but broad-based taxes on certain goods or services, designed with progressive safeguards to protect low-income households, can provide additional revenue without overburdening vulnerable populations. This holistic approach ensures that everyone feels invested in the nation's well-being and future.

Corporations, particularly those that have reaped enormous profits in recent years, must also pay their fair share. Large companies often exploit tax loopholes and regulatory gaps to minimize their obligations, leaving smaller businesses and individual taxpayers to shoulder the burden. By enforcing stricter tax compliance measures, implementing minimum corporate tax rates, and introducing taxes on excessive profits—especially in industries like technology, healthcare, and finance—governments can ensure that corporations contribute equitably to public resources.

The goal of these reforms is not punitive but corrective. In a country of vast wealth, it is both moral and practical to ensure that every citizen has access to the opportunities and resources they need to thrive. Investments in healthcare, education, and housing are not just social goods; they are economic imperatives. Healthy, educated, and secure populations drive innovation, productivity, and growth, creating a virtuous cycle that benefits everyone—including the wealthy and corporations.

Reducing national debt is another critical aspect of progressive tax reform. As the richest nation on Earth, the United States should not find itself grappling with mounting deficits that undermine its ability to invest in the future. By broadening the tax base and ensuring that contributions are proportionate to wealth and income, the country can reduce its reliance on borrowing while still funding ambitious programs. This approach not only secures economic stability but also protects future generations from inheriting an unsustainable financial burden.

A progressive tax system that demands more from those who have the most while ensuring fairness for all is not just about raising revenue—it's about affirming the values of equity, justice, and shared responsibility. By committing to these principles, the United States can move closer to a society where opportunity and prosperity are not privileges reserved for the few, but rights accessible to all. Such a shift requires bold action and a willingness to embrace the collective good over individual gain, but the rewards—a stronger, more cohesive, and more just society—are well worth the effort.

One of the biggest obstacles to building solidarity is the narrative that pits different groups against each other. Racial and

116

cultural divisions are often emphasized in public discourse, distracting from the systemic factors that perpetuate inequality. This narrative benefits the wealthy elite, as it prevents marginalized groups from uniting around shared economic interests.

In reality, poor White and Black Americans face many of the same struggles. Both groups contend with stagnant wages, unaffordable housing, and limited access to healthcare. Yet, these shared challenges are often overshadowed by divisive identity politics that frame economic struggles as zero-sum battles. Overcoming this narrative requires a conscious effort to focus on commonalities rather than differences.

By emphasizing shared experiences and working toward collective solutions, communities can build the solidarity needed to address systemic inequality. This doesn't mean ignoring the unique challenges faced by different groups, but rather recognizing that these challenges are interconnected and require unified action.

Building a more equitable society requires rethinking the systems that underpin economic inequality. By decoupling basic needs like healthcare and housing from capitalism, we can create a framework that prioritizes human dignity and opportunity. A mixed system that combines the strengths of market-driven economies with the guarantees of social safety nets offers a path forward.

This vision of equity is not just about policy—it's about people. Grassroots movements and community organizations show us that real change begins when individuals come together to demand justice and opportunity for all. By focusing on shared struggles and common goals, we can overcome the divisions that have long held us back.

Economic inequality is a unifying issue, one that transcends race, culture, and geography. Addressing it requires collective action, systemic reform, and a commitment to building bridges rather than walls. Together, we can create a society where opportunity is not a privilege but a right—one where every citizen can thrive, regardless of their circumstances.

Cultural and Social Divides

Cultural and social divides have become defining features of modern society, shaping how people interact, communicate, and perceive one another. These divides go beyond mere differences in opinion or perspective—they represent deeper fractures in the way individuals and communities relate to shared values and collective goals. Understanding these divides is essential to addressing polarization and fostering unity, as they influence not only interpersonal relationships but also the broader social, political, and economic systems that govern our lives.

Cultural values and social identities, once sources of richness and diversity, have increasingly become battlegrounds for division. The values that people hold—whether related to religion, family, tradition, or progress—shape their worldview and influence their political and social behavior. These values, while deeply personal, are often projected onto societal debates, where they clash with opposing perspectives.

Consider the contentious debates over issues like reproductive rights, LGBTQ+ equality, or the role of religion in public life. These issues are rooted in cultural values and are often weaponized in political discourse, creating a "culture war" that divides communities. For instance, debates over same-sex marriage or transgender rights often devolve into polarized narratives, where one side views change as a threat to traditional values, while the other sees resistance as an attack on fundamental human rights.

Social identities—race, gender, religion, and sexual orientation—also play a critical role in shaping these divides. Identity politics, while necessary for advocating for marginalized groups, can sometimes exacerbate divisions by framing societal debates as zero-sum conflicts. When individuals perceive threats to their cultural or social identity, they may retreat into echo chambers or adopt defensive postures, making dialogue and compromise increasingly difficult.

The consequences of these divides are profound. When cultural values and social identities become sources of division rather than unity, the ability to work together toward shared goals is severely diminished. This has far-reaching implications for society, from stalling progress on critical issues to eroding trust in institutions and one another.

For example, the lack of shared cultural goals has hindered collective action on issues like climate change, healthcare reform, and education. These are challenges that require cooperation across political, cultural, and social lines, yet polarization has made such collaboration increasingly rare. Instead of focusing on common challenges, societal debates are often consumed by cultural conflicts that distract from larger, systemic issues.

On a more personal level, cultural and social divides strain relationships within families, communities, and workplaces. Friends and relatives find themselves on opposite sides of ideological debates, with differences in opinion turning into sources of resentment or alienation. These divisions weaken the social fabric, making it harder to build trust and solidarity within communities.

Amid these divides, shared cultural and social goals offer a path forward. A society that values inclusivity and mutual respect can harness its diversity as a strength rather than a source of conflict. By focusing on goals that transcend individual identities—such as eradicating poverty, curing diseases, or addressing global crises—society can redirect its energy toward collective progress.

Shared goals do not require uniformity of thought or belief. Instead, they require a willingness to prioritize the common good over individual differences. This does not mean ignoring cultural or social identities but rather recognizing that these identities can coexist within a framework of shared purpose. For example, addressing healthcare disparities benefits everyone, regardless of race, religion, or political affiliation. Similarly, investing in education creates opportunities for all children, fostering equity and reducing division.

This chapter will explore how cultural and social divides shape polarization and hinder progress. It will examine the underlying dynamics of these divide. It will also highlight the importance of shared goals in overcoming these divides, providing a framework for building a more inclusive and cohesive society.

By the end of this chapter, readers will have a deeper understanding of how cultural and social divides affect every aspect of society, from individual relationships to national policies. More importantly, they will see the potential for unity in diversity and the necessity of shared goals in achieving meaningful progress.

The Absence of Shared Goals

Societies thrive when their people are united by shared goals— ambitions that transcend individual interests and foster a collective sense of purpose. These goals serve as the foundation for collaboration, innovation, and progress. However, when societies lack shared objectives, divisions grow deeper, collective action becomes nearly impossible, and opportunities for advancement are lost. In today's polarized world, the absence of shared societal goals has not only hindered progress but has also exacerbated cultural and social divides, leaving many critical challenges unaddressed. Insert chapter seven text here. Insert chapter seven text here.

History provides powerful examples of what societies can achieve when united by a shared purpose. The Apollo moon landing in 1969 is one such moment. At the height of the Cold War, the United States was deeply divided along political, racial, and social lines. Yet, the goal of putting a man on the moon brought the nation together. It was an achievement born from collective effort—a combination of government initiative, scientific ingenuity, and public support. The Apollo program was not merely a technological milestone; it symbolized what humanity could accomplish when united by a common aspiration.

Similarly, the civil rights movement of the 1960s, while deeply contentious, reflected a shared goal among activists and allies: the pursuit of equality and justice for marginalized communities. Though the journey was fraught with resistance, the collective determination of those who fought for civil rights led to transformative legislation, such as the Civil Rights Act of 1964. These moments of unity remind us that shared goals are not just aspirational—they are achievable and necessary for progress.

In contrast, modern society seems unable to rally around such unifying objectives. While technological advancements and social movements continue to emerge, they often exist in fragmented silos, disconnected from a broader sense of shared purpose. This lack of unity has profound implications for addressing today's most pressing challenges.

is a global crisis that demands urgent and unified action. Yet, in the United States and many other nations, it has become a deeply polarized issue. Rather than focusing on practical solutions to reduce emissions, transition to renewable energy, and mitigate environmental damage, public discourse is dominated by ideological clashes. Some deny the existence of the problem entirely, while others advocate for sweeping reforms that are met with resistance from entrenched interests. The result is a paralysis that prevents meaningful progress, despite the overwhelming scientific consensus on the need for action.

Healthcare is another area where the lack of shared goals is painfully evident. Access to affordable, quality healthcare should be a universal priority, yet it remains one of the most divisive topics in modern politics. Debates over policies like the Affordable Care Act or proposals for universal healthcare often devolve into partisan conflicts, leaving millions of people without adequate coverage. This polarization not only hampers efforts to improve healthcare systems but also deepens mistrust between different political and social groups.

Civil rights, too, continues to be a point of contention rather than a unifying cause. While progress has been made in areas such as marriage equality and workplace protections, issues like racial justice and gender equality remain sources of division. Movements advocating for these causes are often met with resistance, framed as threats to traditional values or existing power structures. Instead of rallying around the idea of equality as a shared societal goal, cultural and political divides perpetuate a cycle of conflict and stagnation.

The absence of shared goals does not just hinder progress—it actively deepens social divides. When communities and individuals cannot agree on basic priorities, it becomes easier to view others as adversaries rather than allies. This fragmentation erodes trust, both in one another and in the institutions meant to serve the public good.

For example, the COVID-19 pandemic highlighted the devastating consequences of a fragmented society. Instead of uniting around the shared goal of saving lives and mitigating the virus's spread, responses were marked by deep divisions. Debates over mask mandates, vaccines, and public health measures reflected broader cultural and political fractures, undermining efforts to combat the pandemic effectively. The U.S. faced significantly higher death rates compared to countries that implemented unified responses. According to Johns Hopkins University, by the end of 2022, the U.S. had one of the highest per capita COVID-19 death rates among developed nations, with over 1.1 million fatalities.

Countries like New Zealand, which emphasized a cohesive national strategy, experienced far fewer deaths and faster recovery periods. In contrast, the U.S. response was hampered by conflicting state and federal policies, misinformation, and partisan resistance to basic public health measures. While New Zealand's government implemented clear lockdowns and maintained public trust through consistent messaging, the U.S. saw widespread protests over mask mandates and vaccine requirements, reflecting a fractured approach to a shared crisis.

This lack of a cohesive national response not only prolonged the pandemic's health and economic impacts but also intensified existing tensions, leaving communities more polarized than before. The divergence in outcomes underscores how fragmented societies struggle to address shared challenges, often with dire consequences.

This pattern of fragmentation extends beyond public health. Efforts to address systemic issues like poverty, education, and housing often fall short because they are overshadowed by ideological conflicts. Policies that could benefit millions are frequently blocked or diluted due to partisan gridlock, leaving those in need without support. As these divisions persist, the ability to tackle big-picture challenges—such as curing cancer or addressing global inequality—becomes increasingly out of reach.

The absence of shared goals creates a self-perpetuating cycle of division. Without a unifying vision, communities become more insular, prioritizing their own needs and perspectives over collective progress. This insularity reinforces stereotypes, biases, and mistrust, making it even harder to find common ground.

Despite these challenges, the potential for shared goals remains. History shows that even deeply divided societies can find common ground when they prioritize the collective good. Reimagining shared goals in today's context requires a shift in mindset—one that emphasizes inclusivity, empathy, and a recognition of our interdependence.

For example, imagine a society united by the goal of curing cancer. Achieving this would require the contributions of scientists, healthcare professionals, policymakers, and everyday citizens from all walks of life. It would necessitate investments in research, education, and healthcare infrastructure, as well as a commitment to equity in access to treatment. Such a goal transcends political ideologies, cultural differences, and social identities, reminding us of our shared humanity and the potential for collective achievement.

Similarly, addressing climate change could become a unifying objective if framed as an opportunity rather than a threat. By focusing on the economic and social benefits of transitioning to renewable energy—such as job creation, improved public health, and energy independence—society could rally around a vision of sustainable progress.

The absence of shared goals is one of the greatest barriers to collective progress in modern society. Without a common sense of purpose, divisions deepen, opportunities are lost, and challenges remain unaddressed. Yet, the potential for unity exists. By reimagining shared goals as inclusive, equitable, and forward-thinking, society can begin to bridge its divides and unlock its full potential.

As we move forward in this chapter, we will explore the cultural and social dynamics that contribute to these divisions, as well as the steps needed to foster a more united and cohesive society. Shared goals are not just aspirations—they are essential for addressing the challenges of our time and building a brighter future for all.

Oppression is not a singular phenomenon. It operates across multiple, overlapping dimensions of identity—such as race, gender, class, and sexual orientation—shaping lives and opportunities in complex and multifaceted ways. Intersectionality, a framework introduced by Kimberlé Crenshaw, allows us to understand how these overlapping systems of oppression create unique challenges for individuals and communities. This analysis reveals not only the specific ways marginalized groups are disadvantaged but also how the broader societal fabric, including majority groups, suffers from these inequities.

For centuries, women have been subjected to systemic discrimination that limited their autonomy and contributions to society. Historically denied basic rights—such as voting, property ownership, and equal education—women were effectively excluded from decision-making processes that shaped the world. These barriers were not uniformly experienced. For example, women of color often faced compounded forms of discrimination, where racial and gender biases intersected to exacerbate their marginalization.

Even in contemporary society, gender inequality remains pervasive, affecting women across all socio-economic levels. Women continue to earn significantly less than men for equivalent work, with the gap being even wider for women of color. Additionally, women are consistently underrepresented in leadership positions, making up only a small fraction of top executives in major corporations. These disparities are not merely ethical issues; they also signify missed opportunities for industries and organizations to harness the benefits of diverse perspectives and innovative thinking.

However, gender inequality also impacts men, often through traditional notions of masculinity that restrict emotional expression and discourage them from seeking help or pursuing roles in caregiving and education. These societal norms contribute to higher rates of mental health challenges, substance abuse, and suicide among men, while also perpetuating gender imbalances in critical professions like nursing and teaching. Men who do not conform to these stereotypes may face stigma, reinforcing rigid gender expectations that limit personal and professional fulfillment.

Additionally, economic and cultural shifts have left some men feeling displaced, particularly in communities reliant on traditional industries like manufacturing. The decline of these jobs and the rise of service and tech sectors have exacerbated feelings of insecurity and resentment, with some perceiving broader gender equality efforts as a threat. These dynamics underscore that systemic inequality harms everyone by reinforcing harmful stereotypes and creating divisions. Addressing these challenges requires dismantling outdated notions of masculinity and fostering inclusive systems that value diverse roles and identities for all genders.

Racial oppression, deeply rooted in historical injustices, continues to shape the opportunities and experiences of many individuals. In the United States, the legacy of slavery, Jim Crow laws, and redlining has created structural barriers that limit access to quality education, affordable housing, and equitable healthcare for Black Americans. These systemic inequities are perpetuated through policies and practices that prioritize the status quo, resulting in cycles of poverty and disenfranchisement.

For Indigenous communities, the scars of forced assimilation, cultural erasure, and land displacement remain evident today. Policies like the Indian Removal Act and the establishment of residential schools severed cultural ties and decimated opportunities for self-determination. The ongoing struggles of Indigenous peoples to reclaim sovereignty and resources highlight how historical oppression has contemporary ramifications.

Yet, a nuanced analysis reveals that racial oppression and systemic disparities impact majority groups as well, albeit in less direct ways. The erosion of trust in institutions, often fueled by visible inequities, undermines the confidence necessary for societal cohesion and effective governance. Economic inequality exacerbates these challenges, creating competition for resources and services that pits communities against one another rather than fostering collaboration. This dynamic not only deepens polarization but also weakens the social fabric, making it harder to address collective challenges or achieve shared goals.

The loss of innovation is another critical consequence of systemic oppression. By excluding marginalized groups from full participation in education, employment, and leadership, society deprives itself of a wealth of perspectives, talents, and ideas that could drive progress. Inequitable resource distribution further compounds this issue, as underfunded schools, inadequate healthcare, and limited economic opportunities stifle potential across entire communities, including majority groups in economically disadvantaged regions. Addressing these disparities is not only a moral imperative but also a strategic necessity for unlocking the collective creativity and problem-solving power needed to advance society as a whole.

LGBTQ+ individuals face systemic discrimination that varies across cultural and geographic contexts. In some countries, same-sex relationships are criminalized, with severe punishments ranging from imprisonment to execution. Even in nations where legal protections exist, LGBTQ+ individuals often encounter barriers to healthcare, employment, and social acceptance.

These inequities deprive society of the full potential of LGBTQ+ individuals in areas ranging from the arts to science and technology. For example, historical figures like Alan Turing—whose contributions to computer science were foundational—faced persecution due to their sexual orientation. How many other brilliant minds have been silenced, marginalized, or excluded due to systemic discrimination?

Moreover, the exclusion of LGBTQ+ perspectives diminishes the richness of cultural and societal discourse. Diversity in experiences and identities fosters creativity, empathy, and problem-solving. Without these contributions, societal progress is stunted.

Intersectionality demonstrates that oppression is not experienced in isolation. A Black LGBTQ+ woman, for instance, navigates a different set of challenges than a White woman or a cisgender Black man. Her experiences are shaped by the interplay of racism, sexism, and homophobia, creating barriers that are unique to her identity. These intersecting forms of oppression are often overlooked by systems that address discrimination in siloed categories, failing to account for the compounded impact on individuals at these crossroads.

This framework also highlights how majority groups are not immune to the consequences of systemic oppression. For example, poor White Americans in rural communities often face economic disenfranchisement, inadequate healthcare, and underfunded schools—challenges that mirror those faced by marginalized urban populations. Policies that prioritize urban and suburban development while neglecting rural areas perpetuate these inequities, leaving entire communities behind.

When systemic oppression targets any group, it creates ripple effects that destabilize society as a whole. Inequities fuel polarization, mistrust, and competition for resources, eroding the social cohesion needed for collective progress. Addressing these issues through an intersectional lens allows for more holistic solutions that benefit everyone.

The systemic oppression of marginalized groups has tangible costs, not just for those directly affected but for society as a whole. By excluding individuals based on race, gender, sexual orientation, or other identities, society loses access to diverse perspectives and talents that drive innovation and progress.

Consider the field of medicine. Historically, women and people of color were often excluded from medical schools and research institutions. Today, these gaps in representation still affect patient care and outcomes. Studies have shown that diverse medical teams provide better care by incorporating a wider range of experiences and cultural competencies. Expanding inclusivity in medicine and other fields can lead to breakthroughs that benefit everyone.

Similarly, inclusive policies in the workplace foster creativity and collaboration, leading to higher productivity and better outcomes. Companies that prioritize diversity have been shown to outperform their peers, both in terms of financial success and employee satisfaction. These findings underscore the broader benefits of addressing inequities and creating opportunities for all individuals to contribute fully to society.

Oppression and exclusion are barriers to societal progress, but they are not insurmountable. Addressing these inequities requires a commitment to systemic change and an intersectional approach that recognizes the interconnectedness of all forms of oppression. This means not only dismantling barriers but also fostering environments where diverse perspectives are valued and celebrated.

Investing in education, healthcare, and economic opportunities for marginalized groups is a crucial step toward unlocking society's full potential. At the same time, addressing the grievances of majority groups—such as rural communities facing economic decline—can build solidarity and reduce divisions. A society that values inclusivity is not only more just but also more resilient, innovative, and capable of tackling the challenges of the future.

By embracing intersectionality, society can move beyond the

binary narratives of "us versus them" and recognize that oppression anywhere harms progress everywhere. Together, we can build a world where everyone has the opportunity to thrive—and where collective success is no longer hindered by exclusion.

Oppression and exclusion are not merely moral failings—they are profound barriers to societal progress. By limiting opportunities for marginalized groups, society undermines its own potential, stifling innovation, creativity, and collaboration. The cost of division is borne not just by those directly affected but by everyone who depends on a thriving, equitable society.

Humanity stands at a crossroads. On one side lies a future marked by division, distrust, and stagnation. On the other, a pathway toward unity, progress, and shared achievement. At the heart of this choice are the cultural and social divides that have fragmented society and hindered our collective potential. The stakes could not be higher. Without unity, we are destined to miss out on transformative advancements—longer, healthier lives, the eradication of poverty, solutions to climate change, and even the potential cure for diseases like cancer. But achieving these milestones requires us to confront the divides that hold us back and commit to the urgent work of bridging them.

The Urgency of Unity

Humanity stands at a crossroads. On one side lies a future marked by division, distrust, and stagnation. On the other, a pathway toward unity, progress, and shared achievement. At the heart of this choice are the cultural and social divides that have fragmented society and hindered our collective potential. The stakes could not be higher. Without unity, we are destined to miss out on transformative advancements—longer, healthier lives, the eradication of poverty, solutions to climate change, and even the potential cure for diseases like cancer. But achieving these milestones requires us to confront the divides that hold us back and commit to the urgent work of bridging them.

The consequences of cultural and social divides are evident in every aspect of modern life. When societies lack shared goals, their ability to collaborate on big-picture challenges is severely diminished. Take healthcare, for example. While billions are spent globally on medical research, systemic inequities and fragmented priorities often prevent breakthroughs from reaching everyone who could benefit. Imagine a world where the brightest minds from every background are empowered to work together, unimpeded by barriers of discrimination or exclusion. How much sooner might we find cures for diseases like cancer or Alzheimer's if all talent was recognized, cultivated, and utilized?

Similarly, the fight against climate change—a global crisis that threatens the very future of our planet—has been stymied by polarization and competing priorities. Instead of uniting around practical solutions, societies are locked in ideological battles that delay meaningful action. These divisions are not just political; they are deeply cultural, rooted in mistrust and a lack of empathy for differing perspectives. The result is a fractured response to one of the most pressing issues of our time.

Even in education, one of the most powerful tools for social mobility and innovation, disparities abound. Marginalized communities, whether urban or rural, are often denied access to quality education due to systemic inequities. This leaves untapped potential across all demographics, depriving society of the innovations and solutions that could emerge from these underserved populations. When we fail to invest equitably in education, we deny ourselves the opportunity to benefit from the full spectrum of human talent.

The divides that fragment society are not just moral failings—they are strategic errors that limit humanity's potential. Consider the possibilities if we were united by shared goals. Advances in medical technology, like artificial intelligence in diagnostics, could lead to early detection and prevention of life-threatening illnesses. Collaborative research on aging could extend lifespans, allowing people to enjoy more fulfilling lives. Unified efforts to combat climate change could preserve ecosystems, reduce natural disasters, and create sustainable energy solutions that benefit everyone.

But beyond the tangible achievements, unity offers something even more profound: happiness and fulfillment. Studies consistently show that societies with lower levels of inequality and higher levels of social trust report greater overall well-being. When people feel valued, included, and connected, they are more likely to lead fulfilling lives and contribute positively to their communities.

The cost of division, on the other hand, is staggering. Polarization doesn't just delay progress—it actively undermines it. Resources are wasted on conflicts that could be resolved through dialogue, and opportunities for collaboration are lost to mistrust and fear. The emotional toll of living in a divided society is equally significant. Anxiety, isolation, and hostility flourish when communities are fractured, robbing individuals of the joy and connection that come from working toward common goals.

To move forward, we must first recognize that unity is not about erasing differences. Cultural diversity, varied perspectives, and differing values are strengths that enrich society. Unity, instead, is about creating a framework where these differences can coexist and contribute to shared objectives. It requires empathy—the willingness to see the humanity in one another—and collaboration rooted in mutual respect.

Bridging cultural and social divides is essential to tackling the challenges that define our era. Whether it's addressing systemic inequities, creating more inclusive institutions, or fostering dialogue across polarized communities, the path forward demands intentional effort. This begins with acknowledging the ways in which our divides are perpetuated—through exclusion, misinformation, and fear—and committing to strategies that build bridges rather than walls.

Empathy is the cornerstone of this effort. When we take the time to understand one another's experiences and perspectives, we open the door to meaningful dialogue. This does not mean agreeing on everything; it means respecting the dignity of those with whom we disagree. Collaboration follows naturally from this understanding, as shared goals become the focal point of collective action.

Shared goals are the antidote to division. They remind us of our interconnectedness and our ability to achieve greatness when we work together. Historically, moments of unity have driven humanity's most significant achievements. The Apollo moon landing, the eradication of smallpox, and the creation of international frameworks like the United Nations are all testaments to what we can accomplish when we prioritize common objectives over individual differences.

Today, the stakes are even higher. The challenges we face— climate change, global inequality, public health crises—are complex and interconnected. Addressing them requires collaboration on an unprecedented scale. Shared goals offer a roadmap for this collaboration, focusing our collective energy on solutions that benefit everyone.

The journey toward unity will not be easy. It requires dismantling systemic barriers, challenging entrenched biases, and rebuilding trust in institutions and one another. But the rewards far outweigh the effort. A united society is one where innovation flourishes, inequities are addressed, and progress becomes the norm rather than the exception.

Our divides may seem insurmountable, but they are not inevitable. The urgency of unity lies in its necessity for survival and success. To address the challenges of our time and unlock our collective potential, we must begin by recognizing the humanity in one another and working toward shared goals. This means embracing the idea that every person—regardless of their background, beliefs, or identity—has something valuable to contribute.

In the next section, we will explore practical tools for depolarization. These strategies are designed to foster empathy, understanding, and collaboration, equipping individuals and communities to bridge divides and work toward a more cohesive future. Together, we can create a society where division gives way to connection, and the full potential of humanity is unleashed.

The work begins now—with each of us. By choosing to listen, to learn, and to act, we can build a future defined not by what separates us but by what unites us. The possibilities are limitless: longer lives, healthier communities, sustainable solutions, and a deeper sense of happiness and fulfillment. The choice is ours to make. Let's choose unity.

Part III: Strategies to Depolarize

"Peace is not the absence of conflict, but the ability to handle conflict by peaceful means."
- Ronald Reagan, 1982

International Inspiration

Unity is a powerful and necessary force for progress. While divisions may feel insurmountable, history demonstrates that even the deepest divides can be bridged through intentional action. Societies have faced rifts born of conflict, inequality, and mistrust, yet many have found ways to overcome them, creating pathways to healing and collaboration. Achieving such transformation is not easy, but it is possible when individuals, communities, and nations commit to strategies that rebuild trust, foster dialogue, and confront systemic barriers to unity.

This section delves into strategies for depolarization, offering practical approaches drawn from real-world successes and lessons. At the heart of these strategies is the understanding that bridging divides requires more than agreement—it demands empathy, accountability, and a shared commitment to creating equitable systems. This is not about erasing differences; it's about creating spaces where diverse perspectives can coexist and contribute to shared goals.

The chapter begins with a global perspective, examining how countries have navigated intense societal fractures and emerged stronger. From South Africa's post-apartheid Truth and Reconciliation Commission to Finland's proactive investments in equality, these examples reveal how intentional frameworks can dismantle distrust and cultivate cohesion. By studying these efforts, we can identify the tools and mindsets necessary to foster unity in our own communities.

Depolarization is not an abstract concept or a distant ideal—it is a tangible process with proven outcomes. As part III unfolds, it will explore the building blocks of unity, from addressing historical injustices to fostering dialogue and collaboration. The journey toward reconciliation and understanding is challenging, but the rewards are profound: stronger communities, more innovative solutions, and a society better equipped to face the challenges of the future.

Through these insights, this chapter invites readers to imagine what is possible when humanity chooses connection over conflict. It is a reminder that while divisions may dominate the present, unity remains within our reach—if we are willing to pursue it with purpose and determination.

South Africa: Truth and Reconciliation Commission

Few nations have experienced the level of institutionalized polarization that South Africa endured during apartheid. For decades, apartheid laws enforced racial segregation and oppression, marginalizing Black South Africans and privileging a White minority. By the time apartheid officially ended in 1994, the country faced immense challenges in rebuilding trust and fostering unity across its deeply divided population.

South Africa's Truth and Reconciliation Commission (TRC), established in 1995, became a cornerstone of its depolarization strategy. Chaired by Archbishop Desmond Tutu, the TRC aimed to create a shared understanding of the past while paving the way for a more inclusive future. Central to its mission was the acknowledgment of historical injustices and the establishment of a factual record of apartheid-era abuses. By providing a platform for both victims and perpetrators to share their experiences, the TRC sought to ensure that the truth could not be distorted or forgotten. This commitment to uncovering objective facts was critical, as it allowed the nation to confront its history with clarity, fostering accountability and creating a foundation for reconciliation. Without a clear and agreed-upon picture of the past, efforts to heal and move forward would have been undermined by denial, revisionism, or unresolved resentment.

Unlike traditional trials, the TRC emphasized reconciliation over punishment, a decision that reflected the delicate and urgent need to move a fractured nation forward. Perpetrators of apartheid-era abuses who fully disclosed their actions were eligible for amnesty, a choice that sparked significant debate both within South Africa and internationally. Critics questioned whether this approach undermined justice by allowing those responsible for heinous crimes to avoid imprisonment. Supporters, however, argued that this framework was essential to breaking the cycles of revenge that had perpetuated violence and mistrust for decades. By creating a process rooted in understanding and healing, rather than retribution, the TRC sought to rebuild the social fabric of South Africa, one thread of trust at a time.

This innovative approach recognized that the ultimate goal of justice is not merely punishment but the restoration of relationships and communities. Through public hearings, victims were given the platform to voice their pain, while perpetrators were compelled to confront the harm they had caused. This mutual exposure fostered a form of accountability that transcended traditional punitive measures, as it forced participants to grapple with the human cost of their actions. The TRC provided an essential space for acknowledgment, a cornerstone of reconciliation, and offered South Africa an opportunity to rebuild its national identity on a foundation of shared truth.

The TRC's impact remains a subject of debate, but its achievements are undeniably profound. While it fell short of eradicating the deep racial and economic disparities entrenched by apartheid, the commission succeeded in guiding South Africa's transition to a more inclusive democracy. By creating a comprehensive and public record of apartheid-era atrocities, the TRC not only preserved historical memory but also created a shared narrative that has been instrumental in reducing tensions and fostering coexistence.

For many victims and survivors, the TRC's acknowledgment of their suffering provided a sense of validation that had long been denied. For others, however, the granting of amnesty to perpetrators felt like an incomplete form of justice, highlighting the inherent complexities of balancing accountability with reconciliation. Despite these criticisms, the TRC's work laid a critical foundation for South Africa's future, offering a roadmap for other nations grappling with their own histories of division and oppression.

The commission's approach underscores the importance of confronting uncomfortable truths as a prerequisite for depolarization. Societies cannot heal if they refuse to acknowledge the injustices of the past. The TRC's emphasis on public hearings and transparency created an environment where those truths could no longer be denied or ignored, fostering accountability on both individual and collective levels. This process demonstrates the necessity of collective reckoning to build a society where historical wounds no longer dictate future divisions.

In contrast, the United States has often struggled to engage in similar self-reflection. While South Africa actively sought to address its history of systemic racism and oppression through public acknowledgment and reconciliation, the U.S. has frequently sidestepped its own painful legacies of slavery, segregation, and systemic inequality. For example, debates around reparations for descendants of enslaved people, the continued racial wealth gap, and the legacy of discriminatory practices like redlining remain unresolved. The absence of a unified national effort to confront these issues has allowed historical injustices to fester, fueling ongoing polarization and distrust among communities.

The reluctance to fully accept and address its past has left the U.S. grappling with significant divisions that undermine social cohesion and progress. Without a shared narrative that acknowledges the systemic harm inflicted on marginalized groups, efforts to heal and unify remain superficial. The lack of a formal mechanism to document and reckon with historical injustices perpetuates cycles of mistrust, making reconciliation and progress even more challenging.

Moreover, the TRC demonstrated that reconciliation requires both accountability and empathy—a delicate but vital balance. Accountability ensures that harm is acknowledged and addressed, while empathy allows for the possibility of forgiveness and healing. Together, these elements can break cycles of resentment and retribution, paving the way for long-term peace. This balance is something the U.S. could greatly benefit from, as its own societal divisions continue to widen, fueled by an unwillingness to fully confront its history.

Perhaps most importantly, the TRC illustrated the value of creating spaces where divided communities can engage with one another, confront their differences, and work toward a shared vision of the future. Its legacy serves as a testament to the power of intentional and courageous efforts to bridge divides, even in the face of deep-seated polarization. As South Africa's experience shows, the road to unity is rarely straightforward, but it is always worth pursuing. For the U.S., adopting a similar framework for addressing its historical and systemic inequities could be a crucial step toward creating a more equitable and unified society.

Germany: Confronting Historical Injustices

Germany's strategy for reconciliation focused on comprehensive education and public accountability. These measures emphasized transparency and an unwavering commitment to acknowledging historical truths, creating a foundation for societal healing.

Germany recognized that ignorance and denial would perpetuate the dangers of extremism. To counter this, it implemented a robust education system that made Holocaust education mandatory. Schools across the country teach students about the Holocaust's historical context, the mechanisms of genocide, and the consequences of unchecked hatred and political polarization. This curriculum ensures that young people understand the moral and ethical failures that led to such atrocities and fosters a sense of responsibility to uphold democratic values.

Holocaust education is not treated as a peripheral topic; it is integrated into broader discussions of human rights, the rule of law, and civic engagement. Students are encouraged to engage critically with history, understanding not only what happened but also how and why it happened. This educational approach equips future generations with the tools to identify and resist the conditions that breed hatred and division.

Germany also prioritized public acknowledgment of its past through memorials, museums, and commemorative events. These efforts ensure that the Holocaust remains a visible and inescapable part of the national conscience. Sites like the Memorial to the Murdered Jews of Europe in Berlin, the Dachau concentration camp memorial, and the Jewish Museum serve as constant reminders of the atrocities committed during the Nazi era.

Public memorials and commemorations create spaces for reflection and dialogue, fostering accountability and preventing the erasure or distortion of history. They also symbolize Germany's commitment to transparency, signaling to both its citizens and the world that it will not shy away from confronting its darkest chapters.

Germany's leaders have reinforced this commitment through speeches and policies. For instance, former Chancellor Angela Merkel repeatedly emphasized the importance of remembrance and accountability, urging citizens to remain vigilant against the resurgence of extremism.

Germany's commitment to education and remembrance has made it a global leader in addressing historical injustices. While challenges persist, particularly with the rise of far-right movements in recent years, the nation has cultivated a culture of accountability and vigilance against extremism. By prioritizing education and public acknowledgment, Germany has created a framework for societal healing that other countries can learn from.

However, the German approach also highlights stark contrasts with how some nations, such as the United States, address their own histories of systemic injustice. While Germany has embraced transparency, the U.S. has often struggled to confront its past openly and honestly. For instance, recent debates over school curricula and banned books that address the history of slavery, segregation, and systemic racism reveal deep discomfort with acknowledging the realities of its past. These actions not only hinder progress but also perpetuate divisions, as the refusal to teach or discuss difficult histories prevents society from learning from its mistakes.

In several states across the U.S., books that explore systemic racism, the civil rights movement, or the lived experiences of marginalized groups have been removed from school libraries or curricula. This contrasts sharply with Germany's embrace of education as a tool for accountability and healing. The absence of comprehensive historical education in the U.S. has contributed to ongoing polarization, as communities lack a shared understanding of the injustices that continue to shape the nation.

The German model demonstrates that reckoning with the past is not just about acknowledging wrongdoing—it's about creating a shared narrative that fosters unity and collective progress. By addressing its history transparently, Germany has shown that it is possible to rebuild trust and create a society that values inclusion and accountability. The U.S., by contrast, risks deepening its divisions by failing to fully confront and teach its own history of oppression and inequality.

The lessons from Germany underscore the importance of education and public accountability in preventing polarization and promoting healing. Nations that refuse to confront their past are doomed to repeat its mistakes. In contrast, those that embrace transparency and dialogue create the conditions for a more inclusive and resilient future. Germany's approach illustrates that while the road to reconciliation is long and complex, it is essential for building a society where unity and progress can thrive.

Rwanda: Restoring Unity After Genocide

Rwanda faced one of the most devastating and rapid genocides in modern history. In just 100 days during 1994, nearly one million people were killed, primarily Tutsis targeted by Hutu extremists. The violence was not only staggering in scale but also deeply personal, as neighbors, coworkers, and even family members turned against one another. This horrific conflict, rooted in decades of colonial favoritism, ethnic divisions, and political manipulation, left the nation in ruins—economically, socially, and psychologically.

The genocide did more than claim lives; it destroyed trust among communities, shattered families, and left a legacy of trauma that seemed impossible to overcome. Rwanda faced the monumental task of rebuilding a society where perpetrators and victims would have to live side by side. The challenge was clear: how could a nation so deeply scarred by division heal and move forward?

Recognizing that traditional justice systems would be overwhelmed by the scale of the atrocities, Rwanda adopted innovative approaches that emphasized accountability, healing, and unity.

To address the overwhelming number of crimes, Rwanda established Gacaca courts, a community-based justice system rooted in traditional Rwandan practices. These courts were designed to bring justice closer to the people by involving local communities in the judicial process. Perpetrators were encouraged to confess their actions, seek forgiveness, and receive community-based sentences such as reparations or community service.

The Gacaca courts prioritized restorative justice over punitive measures. While they were not without flaws—critics pointed to inconsistencies and the potential for intimidation—they provided a platform for accountability and dialogue. By involving both victims and perpetrators in the process, the courts aimed to rebuild trust and foster a sense of closure.

Beyond justice, Rwanda's government created the Unity and Reconciliation Commission to promote national healing and

143

prevent future divisions. The commission emphasized a shared national identity, encouraging citizens to think of themselves as "Rwandans first" rather than as Hutus or Tutsis.

Programs included public education campaigns, community-building initiatives, and dialogues that addressed the root causes of division. The government also implemented policies that banned the use of ethnic labels in official documentation and public discourse, reinforcing the idea of national unity.

Rwanda's reconciliation efforts have yielded remarkable progress. The country has experienced rapid economic growth, becoming a model for development in Africa. Infrastructure has been rebuilt, healthcare and education systems have expanded, and poverty rates have significantly declined. More importantly, Rwanda has cultivated a renewed sense of national identity, with many citizens embracing the idea of unity over division.

However, challenges remain. Critics argue that the government's emphasis on national unity sometimes suppresses open discussion about lingering grievances. The balance between reconciliation and free expression continues to be delicate, but Rwanda's progress demonstrates the potential of inclusive and innovative approaches to rebuilding fractured societies.

The Rwandan experience holds valuable lessons for other nations grappling with deep-seated divisions, including the United States. While the U.S. has not experienced genocide on the scale of Rwanda, its history of racial injustice, systemic inequality, and political polarization highlights the need for reconciliation. The idea of grassroots justice and national healing can be adapted to American contexts, addressing long-standing issues such as the legacy of slavery, systemic racism, and the erasure of Indigenous histories.

For example, the Gacaca courts demonstrate the power of community-based justice. In the U.S., localized initiatives that bring together communities to address historical and systemic harm—such as reparative justice programs or truth-telling commissions—could provide a pathway for accountability and healing. These efforts could address racial disparities in policing, housing, and education, fostering understanding and trust among diverse groups.

Similarly, Rwanda's emphasis on promoting a shared national identity offers insights into overcoming polarization. While the U.S. prides itself on diversity, political and cultural divides often overshadow this strength. A focus on shared goals and values—such as equality, opportunity, and justice—could help bridge divides and create a more cohesive society. Programs that encourage cross-cultural dialogue and collaboration could reinforce the idea that Americans, despite their differences, are united in their aspirations for a better future.

Rwanda's progress is a testament to the resilience of the human spirit and the power of collective action. While no system is perfect, the nation's commitment to addressing its past, fostering accountability, and building a shared future offers hope and inspiration. For the U.S., embracing these lessons could pave the way for a more inclusive and unified society. The challenges are significant, but as Rwanda has shown, the possibilities are transformative when a nation chooses to confront its divisions head-on.

Finland: Building Trust Through Equality

Unlike nations grappling with historical injustices or deep-rooted ethnic conflicts, Finland has not faced severe historical polarization. However, it has recognized the potential for divisions to emerge in any society and has taken proactive steps to prevent them. As globalization, migration, and technological change reshape societies worldwide, Finland's emphasis on trust, equality, and inclusivity offers a compelling model for fostering societal cohesion and resilience.

Finland's education system is a cornerstone of its efforts to build an equitable society. Widely regarded as one of the most effective in the world, Finland's approach focuses on eliminating disparities and ensuring that all children, regardless of their background, have access to high-quality education.

Finland's education system is a cornerstone of its efforts to build an equitable society. Widely regarded as one of the most effective in the world, Finland's approach focuses on eliminating disparities and ensuring that all children, regardless of their background, have access to high-quality education.

Key features include free education at all levels, from primary school through university, and comprehensive support systems for students. Schools provide free meals, access to healthcare, and counseling services, ensuring that socioeconomic factors do not hinder learning. Moreover, Finland's teachers are highly trained and respected professionals, equipped to address the diverse needs of their students.

The emphasis on individualized learning plans allows educators to meet students where they are, helping each child reach their potential. By creating an environment where students feel supported and valued, Finland cultivates a sense of inclusion and belonging from an early age, reducing the risk of future societal divisions.

In addition to its world-renowned education system, Finland's universal healthcare and social welfare programs play a critical role in addressing economic disparities. These initiatives ensure that all citizens have access to essential resources such as medical care, housing, and income support. By removing barriers to these basic necessities, Finland creates a sense of collective security that mitigates the economic anxieties often found in more unequal societies. This framework promotes social cohesion by reinforcing the idea that everyone, regardless of their background, is entitled to a baseline standard of living.

A cornerstone of this approach is Finland's healthcare system, which provides equal access to medical services for all citizens, regardless of their financial status or geographical location. Funded primarily through taxation, the system ensures that no one is left without care due to an inability to pay. Municipalities organize and deliver healthcare services, allowing for localized solutions that meet the specific needs of communities. By prioritizing equity in healthcare, Finland eliminates disparities in outcomes and fosters trust in public institutions. This equitable access not only improves individual well-being but also strengthens the overall resilience of Finnish society.

Complementing its healthcare system, Finland's social welfare programs provide comprehensive support to its citizens. Unemployment benefits offer financial security during periods of joblessness, while child allowances help families manage the costs of raising children. Housing subsidies ensure that individuals and families have access to stable and affordable living conditions. These programs go beyond addressing immediate needs; they serve as an investment in long-term societal well-being. By reducing poverty and economic insecurity, Finland's welfare system creates an environment where individuals can focus on contributing to society rather than merely surviving. This integrated approach to healthcare and social welfare underscores Finland's commitment to equity and its belief in the value of investing in its people.

Finland's approach has yielded impressive results. The country consistently ranks among the happiest and most equitable nations in the world. Its citizens report high levels of trust in institutions, a factor closely linked to social cohesion and stability. By ensuring that basic needs are met and opportunities are accessible to all, Finland has cultivated a culture of trust, shared responsibility, and collaboration.

The Finnish experience highlights the transformative power of investing in equality. By reducing disparities and fostering inclusivity, societies can prevent the polarization and resentment that often arise from economic and social inequality. This approach not only strengthens social cohesion but also enhances collective well-being and resilience in the face of global challenges.

Finland's success underscores a critical insight: polarization is not inevitable. Societies can choose to invest in systems and policies that foster equality and trust, reducing the conditions that lead to division. By focusing on shared goals and ensuring that all citizens feel included and supported, nations can build resilient and cohesive communities capable of addressing collective challenges.

In stark contrast, the United States has often struggled to

adopt similar measures. Despite being one of the wealthiest nations in the world, the U.S. lacks universal healthcare, leaving millions without access to affordable medical services. The absence of a comprehensive social safety net means that many Americans face economic insecurity that could be alleviated by policies akin to Finland's unemployment benefits, child allowances, or housing subsidies. Instead, fragmented and underfunded programs leave significant gaps, exacerbating inequality and fostering resentment among those who feel left behind.

Moreover, the U.S. education system often reflects and perpetuates socioeconomic disparities. Unlike Finland's model of equitable access, American public schools are largely funded by local property taxes, resulting in stark differences in resources between affluent and low-income areas. These disparities create barriers to opportunity for millions of students, undermining social mobility and deepening societal divides. In contrast, Finland's emphasis on equity in education ensures that all children, regardless of their background, have a fair shot at success.

The lack of shared goals further compounds these challenges in the U.S. While Finland invests in policies that create collective security and foster unity, American political discourse is often characterized by divisions that hinder progress on critical issues. Polarization over healthcare, climate change, and economic reform has stymied efforts to implement systemic changes that could benefit the entire population. Instead of addressing structural inequalities, the focus on ideological battles has widened the gaps between communities, eroded trust in institutions, and left pressing problems unaddressed.

As countries around the world grapple with rising inequality, cultural tensions, and political polarization, Finland's model serves as a reminder that unity is achievable when equality and inclusivity are prioritized. The Finnish example invites societies to ask: What kind of future do we want to build, and how can we ensure that no one is left behind in the process? For the United States, answering this question requires confronting its systemic inequities head-on and embracing policies that prioritize the well-being of all citizens. Without such a shift, the divisions that currently plague American society are likely to deepen, further hindering the nation's ability to address collective challenges and achieve shared progress.

Shared Goals

The experiences of Finland, Germany, South Africa, and Rwanda offer critical lessons for addressing polarization, fostering unity, and investing in shared goals. Each of these nations faced unique challenges, yet they found ways to prioritize inclusion, reconciliation, and social equity. Their successes, as well as their ongoing struggles, provide a roadmap for nations like the United States to confront its own deep divisions and systemic inequities.

The common thread running through the experiences of Finland, Germany, South Africa, and Rwanda is the intentional investment in addressing deep divisions by fostering inclusion, accountability, and a sense of shared purpose. While each nation faced unique challenges, their successes highlight universal strategies that transcend borders. Their lessons collectively underscore the importance of building equity, confronting history, fostering dialogue, and prioritizing unity.

Equity is foundational to social cohesion, as demonstrated by Finland's proactive investments in universal education, healthcare, and social welfare. By reducing economic disparities and ensuring that all citizens have access to basic necessities, Finland has created a society where trust in institutions and among individuals flourishes. Universal systems like free education and healthcare mitigate the inequalities that often lead to resentment and division, fostering a culture where everyone feels valued.

This focus on equity is echoed in the policies of Germany, South Africa, and Rwanda, albeit in different forms. Germany's reparations and investments in Holocaust education demonstrate an effort to provide equity not only in material terms but also in narrative and memory, ensuring that past injustices are addressed. Similarly, South Africa's TRC provided victims of apartheid-era abuses with a platform to seek recognition and justice, offering a form of moral equity that acknowledged their suffering. Rwanda's grassroots Gacaca courts sought to balance justice with healing, ensuring that even the most devastated communities had a voice in rebuilding their nation.

For the U.S., the lesson is clear: equity must be prioritized. Economic inequality, racial disparities, and systemic injustices continue to erode trust and cohesion. Addressing these challenges requires universal solutions that ensure all citizens have access to resources and opportunities, reinforcing the shared belief that everyone has a stake in the nation's future.

Acknowledging and addressing historical injustices is another shared theme. Germany's mandatory Holocaust education and public memorials have created a collective understanding of the nation's darkest chapters. By preserving historical memory, Germany prevents the erasure or distortion of its past, fostering accountability and vigilance against the resurgence of extremism.

South Africa's Truth and Reconciliation Commission took a similar approach, prioritizing public acknowledgment of apartheid-era atrocities. By giving victims a platform to share their experiences and granting amnesty to perpetrators who fully disclosed their actions, South Africa confronted its history head-on. This commitment to transparency helped lay the groundwork for a more inclusive democracy.

The U.S. has much to learn from these examples. While Germany and South Africa embraced the discomfort of reckoning with their pasts, the U.S. continues to struggle with systemic racism, Indigenous erasure, and the legacy of slavery. Debates over how to teach this history in schools, including bans on books that address systemic racism, highlight the nation's reluctance to confront its past. Without a shared understanding of its history, the U.S. risks perpetuating divisions and undermining efforts to build a cohesive future.

Open dialogue is another critical element shared by these nations. South Africa's TRC and Rwanda's Gacaca courts created spaces for divided communities to come together, confront their differences, and work toward healing. While these processes were far from perfect, they demonstrated the transformative power of communication and restorative justice.

Both nations emphasized the importance of grassroots solutions. In South Africa, community hearings allowed victims and perpetrators to engage directly, fostering empathy and understanding. Rwanda's Gacaca courts, though criticized for inconsistencies, empowered communities to participate in justice and reconciliation, reinforcing the idea that healing begins at the local level.

The U.S. would benefit from adopting similar approaches. Community-based initiatives, such as truth-telling commissions and reparative justice programs, could address systemic inequalities and foster understanding across racial, cultural, and political divides. Creating spaces for dialogue at the grassroots level would help rebuild trust and pave the way for broader societal healing.

All four nations demonstrate the importance of prioritizing unity. Whether through Finland's investments in social equity, Germany's acknowledgment of historical injustices, South Africa's reconciliation efforts, or Rwanda's emphasis on shared identity, each nation has worked to foster a sense of collective purpose. Unity does not mean erasing differences; rather, it involves creating a framework where diverse voices and perspectives are valued and contribute to a common goal.

For the U.S., the lesson is to move beyond divisions and focus on shared goals that benefit all citizens. Addressing economic inequality, investing in education and healthcare, and combating climate change are examples of unifying objectives that transcend partisan lines. By framing these challenges as collective endeavors, the U.S. can foster a sense of shared purpose that strengthens its social fabric.

Shared Goals We Need to Invest In

To address polarization and build a more inclusive society, the U.S. must focus on shared goals that transcend individual identities and ideological divides. These goals should prioritize the well-being of all citizens and reflect the collective aspirations of the nation, providing a roadmap toward unity and progress.

Investing in equitable education is essential to fostering upward mobility and reducing systemic inequalities. Disparities in public school funding must be addressed to ensure that all children, regardless of their socioeconomic background, have access to quality education. Affordable higher education and opportunities for lifelong learning should also be prioritized. Education has the power to unite by equipping every citizen with the tools they need to succeed and contribute meaningfully to society.

Healthcare reform is another cornerstone of creating a more equitable society. Access to affordable healthcare is a fundamental human right and a vital step toward achieving social equity. A universal healthcare system, inspired by successful models like Finland's, would help reduce disparities in health outcomes and provide a safety net for all Americans. Such reform should emphasize preventive care, mental health services, and affordable medications to ensure holistic well-being for the entire population.

Economic justice is critical to addressing the growing wealth gap that has left many Americans behind. The U.S. must implement progressive tax reforms, raise the minimum wage, and strengthen labor protections to create a more equitable economy. Targeted investments in affordable housing, childcare, and job training programs would empower low- and middle-income families while fostering economic stability and growth. These initiatives would not only address material disparities but also help build trust and cohesion within society.

Climate action stands out as a shared goal that transcends political boundaries. The U.S. must invest in renewable energy, sustainable infrastructure, and environmental conservation to combat this global crisis. Policies should focus on marginalized communities disproportionately affected by environmental degradation, ensuring that no one is left behind in the pursuit of sustainability. By addressing climate change collaboratively, the nation can foster unity and demonstrate the power of shared responsibility.

Finally, rebuilding trust in institutions and promoting civic engagement are essential to reducing polarization. Electoral reforms, such as expanding voting access, addressing gerrymandering, and ensuring transparency in campaign financing, can strengthen democratic norms and create a more inclusive political system. Programs that encourage civic participation and dialogue across divides can help bridge gaps and foster a sense of unity.

By prioritizing these shared goals—education, healthcare, economic justice, climate action, and democratic renewal—the U.S. can begin to address the systemic issues that fuel polarization. These efforts will create a foundation for a society that values equity, collaboration, and shared progress, paving the way for a brighter and more united future.

The path to addressing polarization and fostering a more inclusive society lies in our collective commitment to shared goals that transcend individual identities and divisions. Whether through equitable education, universal healthcare, economic justice, climate action, or revitalizing democratic engagement, these priorities represent the building blocks of a society rooted in trust, fairness, and unity. The examples of nations like Finland, Germany, South Africa, and Rwanda remind us that progress is not only possible but achievable when communities confront their challenges with transparency, collaboration, and a commitment to equity.

As we conclude this chapter, it is essential to recognize that these goals are not lofty ideals reserved for distant futures; they are practical, necessary steps that can create real, transformative change. A society that invests in its people—ensuring that every individual feels valued and supported—becomes a society capable of addressing the monumental challenges of our time. The next section will explore the tools and strategies to depolarize and bridge divides, empowering us to take those first critical steps toward a future where unity and shared purpose drive progress.

Reconciliation

Reconciliation is not just a concept—it's an essential process for repairing the fractures within our society. Over time, polarization, whether political, cultural, or economic, has entrenched divisions that seem impossible to overcome. These divides are evident in our relationships, communities, and institutions, stifling progress and collaboration. Yet history and research demonstrate that reconciliation is not only possible but transformative when approached with intention and commitment. At its core, reconciliation is rooted in understanding, healing, and collaboration—a framework for addressing long-standing divides and building a unified future.

This chapter serves as a foundation for understanding the necessity of reconciliation and the steps required to achieve it. It emphasizes that reconciliation is both a personal and collective journey, requiring individuals and communities to confront uncomfortable truths and foster empathy and mutual respect. By exploring actionable strategies such as fostering empathy through storytelling, addressing systemic inequalities, and reforming education, this chapter highlights how reconciliation can bridge divides and serve as a powerful tool for societal progress.

Reconciliation is often misconstrued as a passive act of forgiveness or a quiet acceptance of the past. In reality, it is a dynamic and transformative process that actively seeks to create understanding where mistrust existed, healing where pain lingered, and collaboration where division persisted. It involves acknowledging historical and ongoing injustices, addressing grievances, and laying the groundwork for mutual respect and shared objectives.

In today's polarized world, reconciliation plays an even more critical role. Political ideologies, economic disparities, and cultural differences have hardened into entrenched divides, creating an environment where progress feels unattainable. Reconciliation provides a structured approach to dismantling these barriers. It invites dialogue and collaboration, recognizing that unresolved grievances perpetuate cycles of mistrust and hostility. By fostering this understanding, reconciliation creates the conditions necessary for meaningful and sustainable unity.

Reconciliation starts with personal accountability, a responsibility each of us must embrace to bridge divides. It requires us to look inward, examining our biases, assumptions, and how we may have contributed to existing tensions. This isn't easy—self-reflection often brings discomfort and challenges our defensive instincts. But to move forward, we must confront where we've been complicit or passive in perpetuating harm, acknowledging that reconciliation is not a passive process but an active, deliberate effort.

Empathy is the heart of this journey. It transforms abstract disagreements into human connections, helping us see others as complex individuals rather than stereotypes or adversaries. Storytelling initiatives and dialogue circles create vital spaces where people from different backgrounds and beliefs can share their lived experiences. These moments of honest exchange have the power to dismantle prejudice and build understanding, providing a pathway for both personal growth and broader societal healing. They remind us that reconciliation is not about agreeing on everything but about understanding and respecting the humanity in one another.

Now is the time to act. Begin by listening—seek out stories that challenge your perspective. Participate in community dialogues or take steps to educate yourself about the experiences of those different from you. Empathy and accountability are not abstract ideals; they are daily practices that, when embraced collectively, lay the foundation for a more unified society. By committing to this personal work, we become active participants in the larger process of reconciliation, demonstrating that change starts not with others but with ourselves.

While personal accountability lays the groundwork for reconciliation, the process must also scale to encompass communities and entire societies. Collective reconciliation requires addressing systemic issues that create and sustain division, including economic inequality, systemic racism, and gender disparities. These systemic challenges cannot be solved through individual efforts alone—they demand structured spaces for dialogue, institutional acknowledgment of harm, and mechanisms that validate the experiences of those who have been wronged. The goal is not only to confront injustices but also to foster understanding and collaboration that pave the way for long-term healing.

History provides compelling examples of how collective reconciliation can succeed when approached with intentionality. South Africa's Truth and Reconciliation Commission created a platform for victims and perpetrators to openly share their experiences, allowing the country to acknowledge the profound harm of apartheid and begin the process of healing. Similarly, Rwanda's Gacaca courts, rooted in community participation, provided an avenue for accountability and forgiveness following the devastating genocide. Both initiatives highlighted the importance of creating shared narratives—stories that validate the suffering of victims while encouraging perpetrators to take responsibility for their actions. These efforts, while imperfect, underline the necessity of public acknowledgment and shared dialogue in breaking cycles of mistrust and resentment.

For the United States, these lessons are particularly relevant. The deep scars left by slavery, Indigenous displacement, and systemic inequities continue to shape the nation's divisions today. Without structured efforts to address these injustices—through truth-telling initiatives, reparative justice programs, or educational reforms—healing remains elusive. Collective reconciliation is not about assigning blame but about creating a shared understanding of the past as a foundation for moving forward. It challenges societies to confront uncomfortable truths, validate diverse experiences, and actively work toward a more equitable and unified future. The examples of South Africa and Rwanda show that even the deepest divisions can be bridged through commitment, empathy, and the courage to engage in honest dialogue.

Reconciliation is not without its challenges. It requires confronting uncomfortable truths, which can be deeply unsettling, particularly for those who benefit from existing systems of power and privilege. Acknowledging harm often brings discomfort, as it forces individuals and institutions to reckon with the ways in which they have perpetuated inequities. Fear of change, resistance to accountability, and the emotional weight of revisiting trauma are significant barriers to progress. These hurdles may seem insurmountable, but history and experience show that, with intention and empathy, they can be overcome.

Reconciliation is not only about addressing harm but also about unlocking the potential of collaboration. When trust is restored and divides are bridged, societies can achieve remarkable progress. Consider the transformative power of unity in tackling global challenges such as curing diseases, combating climate change, or advancing technological innovation. When voices from diverse backgrounds come together, they contribute unique insights and approaches, enriching solutions in ways that homogeneity cannot. Reconciliation allows for the dismantling of barriers that stifle creativity and innovation, creating environments where every person's potential can be realized. In essence, reconciliation is the foundation for a society that values inclusion, creativity, and progress over division and exclusion.

The process of reconciliation is not a singular event but a continuous effort that involves systemic change, education, and personal accountability. Addressing harm requires dismantling the structures that uphold inequality, such as discriminatory policies or economic disparities. Education plays a vital role in fostering understanding, as it equips individuals with the tools to empathize with others' experiences and challenge their own biases. Personal accountability, meanwhile, is essential for creating a culture of introspection and growth. Together, these components form a cohesive strategy for achieving reconciliation and building a society that thrives on mutual respect and shared goals.

In this chapter and its sections, we will address these challenges one by one, breaking down the barriers to reconciliation and exploring actionable steps for individuals, communities, and institutions. Each section delves into a different aspect of the reconciliation process, from fostering empathy through storytelling to implementing systemic reforms. While the path is not easy, it is essential. Reconciliation is the bridge that can carry us from division to unity, from stagnation to progress. Together, we will explore how to confront these challenges, embrace the possibilities of reconciliation, and build a future grounded in understanding, equity, and shared goals.

Resistance to Accountability

Reconciliation often falters at its first hurdle: accountability. For many individuals and institutions, the concept of accountability is perceived as synonymous with punishment or loss. This fear can manifest as defensiveness, denial, or outright rejection of reconciliation efforts. Such resistance poses a significant challenge, as accountability is a cornerstone of genuine reconciliation. Without it, efforts to bridge divides and heal communities remain superficial, failing to address the root causes of division and harm.

Accountability requires individuals and institutions to confront uncomfortable truths about their roles in perpetuating harm or inequality. This process can threaten entrenched power dynamics, as it often involves redistributing power, acknowledging privilege, or admitting wrongdoing. For those who benefit from existing systems, accountability may feel like a threat to their social status or economic security. This fear frequently leads to resistance, undermining reconciliation initiatives before they can gain traction.

In the United States, resistance to acknowledging systemic racism offers a clear example of this challenge. Debates over how race and history are taught in schools illustrate how accountability is often avoided. Efforts to include comprehensive curricula about slavery, segregation, and systemic inequities are met with accusations of "divisiveness" or "indoctrination." This defensiveness often stems from a reluctance to confront the ways in which systemic racism has shaped modern institutions and opportunities.

Similarly, corporations and institutions often resist accountability for environmental damage. Companies responsible for pollution or deforestation frequently deflect blame, deny responsibility, or engage in performative gestures that lack substantive change. The fear of financial repercussions, public backlash, or regulatory consequences motivates this resistance, highlighting how power and privilege can act as barriers to reconciliation.

In the United States, attempts to incorporate discussions of systemic racism into school curricula have faced significant opposition. Critics often label such lessons as "divisive" or "anti-American," arguing that they undermine national unity (the irony of which is not missed on me). Legislative bans on teaching critical race theory (CRT), enacted or proposed in several states, exemplify this pushback. However, CRT is primarily taught at the graduate level and is rarely included in K-12 curricula. These bans often conflate CRT with broader efforts to address the historical and ongoing impacts of racism in the U.S. According to a report by PEN America, these restrictions create a chilling effect on educators, who may feel unable to discuss crucial aspects of American history, such as slavery, segregation, and civil rights struggles.

This resistance is fundamentally a refusal to take accountability for the systemic inequities that have shaped the nation's past and continue to influence its present. By rejecting discussions of racism's historical roots and its modern manifestations, society denies itself the opportunity to fully understand the causes of racial disparities in education, housing, healthcare, and economic mobility. Without this understanding, policy responses to these disparities remain superficial, addressing symptoms rather than root causes. For example, efforts to improve school funding or address housing inequities will falter if they do not consider the structural barriers created by discriminatory practices like redlining or segregation.

Avoiding accountability in this way perpetuates cycles of inequality and division. It also undermines critical thinking and empathy—skills essential for fostering an inclusive and equitable society. An accurate and inclusive curriculum allows students to understand the complexity of historical and contemporary issues, preparing them to engage thoughtfully with the challenges of the present. Moreover, confronting uncomfortable truths is not inherently divisive; it is a necessary step toward unity. By acknowledging past and ongoing injustices, society can begin to address them collectively, fostering mutual understanding and a shared commitment to progress.

The reluctance to take accountability in this context is not just an academic or ideological issue—it has real, tangible consequences. When educators are restricted from teaching about systemic racism, students lose the opportunity to develop a nuanced understanding of history and its implications for modern society. This not only limits their ability to critically analyze the world around them but also perpetuates ignorance and misunderstanding among future generations. In a diverse society, failing to provide young people with the tools to engage with differing perspectives creates a fragile foundation for national unity. Reconciliation and progress require courage, honesty, and a willingness to confront the past, even when it is uncomfortable. Without these, societal divisions will continue to deepen, making collective progress increasingly difficult.

Resistance to accountability in the corporate world, particularly regarding environmental harm, exemplifies a profound failure to confront systemic challenges. By engaging in greenwashing rather than implementing substantive changes, companies deflect responsibility and undermine the broader effort to combat climate change. This is not true accountability—it is a performative facade that delays meaningful progress. Highlighting small investments in renewable energy while continuing to prioritize fossil fuel production allows corporations to maintain the status quo, perpetuating environmental degradation and reinforcing public mistrust.

This refusal to take full accountability has tangible and far-reaching consequences. For one, it exacerbates environmental injustice. Communities near industrial facilities—often low-income neighborhoods or communities of color—bear the brunt of the pollution generated by corporate practices. These areas frequently experience higher rates of respiratory illnesses, cardiovascular diseases, and other health issues linked to poor air quality. Despite their public sustainability commitments, corporations often fail to address these disparities, leaving the most vulnerable populations to suffer. The Environmental Protection Agency (EPA) has repeatedly documented how these systemic inequities disproportionately affect marginalized communities, further entrenching cycles of inequality and mistrust.

The problem extends beyond environmental harm to erode public trust in institutions and the private sector's ability—or willingness—to be part of the solution. When companies prioritize image over impact, they create skepticism about the feasibility of tackling climate change and other global challenges. This deflection not only delays necessary reforms but also discourages collective action by presenting the illusion that sufficient efforts are already underway. True accountability would require these corporations to align their practices with their public commitments, investing significantly in renewable energy and adopting measures to mitigate the harm they cause.

The failure to take accountability represents a missed opportunity to drive meaningful change. Corporations hold significant resources and influence, which, if wielded responsibly, could accelerate the transition to a sustainable future. By refusing to fully acknowledge their impact and deflecting scrutiny, they hinder progress not just for themselves but for society as a whole. Addressing this issue requires a combination of stronger regulatory frameworks, transparency mandates, and public pressure to ensure that corporations prioritize environmental justice and sustainability over short-term profits. Real accountability is not about avoiding blame; it is about taking meaningful steps to rectify harm and build a future that benefits everyone.

Resistance to accountability in housing and economic policies exemplifies how entrenched inequities are perpetuated when institutions and policymakers refuse to confront their role in systemic injustices. These inequities have created stark generational wealth gaps that continue to shape disparities in education, employment, and health outcomes. Failing to take accountability for these systemic harms deepens the structural divide and reinforces barriers that limit opportunities for marginalized groups.

For instance, when federal programs like the Affirmatively Furthering Fair Housing (AFFH) rule are rolled back or delayed, it sends a message that addressing historical and ongoing discrimination is not a priority. The AFFH rule, designed to promote equitable opportunities in housing, has faced opposition from administrations wary of the political and economic risks of enforcement. This inaction allows discriminatory practices in housing markets to persist, leaving marginalized communities with fewer pathways to stability and upward mobility. This resistance to change perpetuates cycles of exclusion and prevents the broader society from reaping the benefits of a more equitable housing landscape.

Beyond systemic exclusion, the lack of accountability in housing policies undermines public trust in institutions and reinforces societal divisions. When marginalized populations see that discriminatory practices remain unaddressed, it fosters a sense of disenfranchisement and cynicism toward government and policymakers. This mistrust makes it even harder to build consensus around necessary reforms, further entrenching a status quo that benefits a select few at the expense of the many.

To overcome this resistance, bold leadership and community-driven advocacy are essential. Policymakers must be willing to implement reparative housing policies, enforce anti-discrimination laws, and expand affordable housing initiatives. At the same time, grassroots movements can push for greater transparency and accountability, ensuring that housing reforms center on those most affected by inequality. By addressing these challenges head-on, society can move toward a future where housing is not a privilege for some but a foundational right for all.

One of the most effective ways to overcome this resistance is to reframe accountability as a mutually beneficial process rather than a punitive one. When individuals and institutions recognize that accountability fosters stronger communities, more sustainable systems, and greater trust, they are more likely to engage in reconciliation efforts.

Accountability is not about assigning blame or seeking retribution—it is about creating opportunities for growth, understanding, and collaboration. For example, companies that take responsibility for their environmental impact and invest in sustainable practices often see long-term benefits, including improved public trust, customer loyalty, and financial performance. Similarly, communities that engage in honest conversations about systemic racism often find that these dialogues pave the way for deeper connections and shared progress.

Restorative justice models offer a powerful framework for overcoming resistance to accountability. Unlike traditional punitive approaches, restorative justice emphasizes dialogue, restitution, and healing. This model encourages individuals and institutions to take responsibility for harm in ways that prioritize reconciliation and forward movement.

In practice, restorative justice might involve community forums where affected parties can share their experiences and discuss paths toward resolution. For corporations, this could mean engaging with communities impacted by their actions, funding reparative programs, and committing to transparent sustainability goals. By focusing on restitution and healing, restorative justice allows accountability to feel constructive rather than punitive, reducing the fear that often drives resistance.

Public education campaigns also play a crucial role in fostering a culture of accountability. These campaigns can challenge misconceptions about accountability by highlighting its positive outcomes. For example, storytelling initiatives that showcase communities or companies successfully addressing harm can inspire others to follow suit. By framing accountability as a tool for healing and progress, education campaigns can shift public perception and reduce resistance.

Empathy is a central component of these campaigns. When people understand the lived experiences of those affected by harm—whether through personal stories, documentaries, or community dialogues—they are more likely to support accountability efforts. Empathy transforms accountability from an abstract concept into a tangible necessity, making it easier for individuals and institutions to embrace the process.

To address resistance effectively, societies must also shift the narratives that surround accountability. Current discourse often frames accountability as a zero-sum game, where one party's gain comes at another's loss. This framing reinforces fear and defensiveness, perpetuating cycles of denial and inaction.

By emphasizing shared benefits and collective progress, reconciliation efforts can reframe accountability as a collaborative endeavor. For example, acknowledging and addressing systemic racism is not about blaming individuals—it is about creating opportunities for all communities to thrive. Similarly, holding corporations accountable for environmental harm is not about punishment—it is about ensuring a sustainable future for everyone.

Deep-Seated Mistrust

Mistrust is one of the most persistent and damaging obstacles to reconciliation in polarized societies. Whether rooted in historical grievances, entrenched stereotypes, or political divisions, mistrust poisons the well of dialogue and obstructs progress. For reconciliation to succeed, societies must confront and dismantle this mistrust, recognizing its origins and addressing it through deliberate actions.

Mistrust often stems from broader societal and systemic factors that extend beyond well-known issues of racial discrimination and political polarization. For example, the privatization of essential services like healthcare and education has created disparities that deepen mistrust between socio-economic groups. Many low-income communities view privatized systems as catering to the wealthy while leaving them with substandard options. This mistrust is compounded by a lack of transparency and accountability in how these systems are managed, leading to frustration and disengagement from broader societal structures.

In workplace settings, mistrust emerges when employees feel disconnected from decision-making processes or perceive inequitable treatment. For instance, wage stagnation and disparities in benefits can create a divide between employees and leadership, fostering a culture of suspicion and resentment. When workers see executives prioritizing profits over employee welfare, they may feel undervalued and exploited, further eroding trust in institutions that claim to uphold fairness and opportunity.

Another significant source of mistrust is environmental inequity. Communities located near industrial facilities often experience higher levels of pollution, degraded living conditions, and health issues. The lack of meaningful corporate accountability for environmental harm perpetuates the belief that certain populations—often low-income or rural—are viewed as expendable. This belief is exacerbated by insufficient government intervention, leaving these communities feeling abandoned by both public and private entities. These situations illustrate how mistrust can be fueled by environmental and economic inequities, in addition to social and political divides.

Mistrust is evident in polarized political landscapes, where partisanship overrides opportunities for collaboration. In the

U.S., debates over healthcare, climate change, and voting rights are frequently framed as zero-sum battles, with each side accusing the other of acting in bad faith. For instance, during the COVID-19 pandemic, efforts to implement public health measures like mask mandates and vaccination campaigns were met with widespread mistrust, particularly in politically conservative communities. This resistance was not solely about the measures themselves but reflected deeper suspicions about government overreach and the motivations of public health officials.

In communities with historical grievances, mistrust often hinders reconciliation efforts. For example, truth and reconciliation commissions, such as those in South Africa or Canada, sometimes face criticism from marginalized groups who feel that these initiatives do not go far enough in addressing systemic harms. Indigenous communities in Canada, for instance, have expressed skepticism about the government's commitment to implementing the recommendations of the Truth and Reconciliation Commission, citing a lack of tangible progress on issues like land rights and access to clean water.

Addressing deep-seated mistrust requires a nuanced, multifaceted approach that emphasizes transparency, inclusivity, and incremental progress. While it is impossible to eliminate mistrust overnight, sustained efforts to rebuild trust can pave the way for successful reconciliation and stronger societal bonds. This process hinges on creating safe spaces for dialogue, fostering collaboration through shared goals, and drawing inspiration from successful examples of reconciliation.

Neutral, trusted spaces for dialogue are essential in combating mistrust, as they allow individuals and groups to communicate openly without fear of judgment or retaliation. These spaces must be facilitated by mediators who are widely respected and perceived as impartial. Community centers, faith-based organizations, or independent commissions can serve as venues for such dialogues, offering an environment where participants can share their perspectives and seek common ground.

For instance, the Community Relations Service (CRS) in the

United States, a division of the Department of Justice, has successfully facilitated dialogues in communities grappling with racial or cultural tensions. By engaging diverse stakeholders in structured conversations focused on shared goals, the CRS has helped bridge divides and build trust incrementally. These dialogues have not only addressed immediate conflicts but also established a precedent for collaborative problem-solving. Such efforts highlight the importance of creating intentional spaces where mistrust can be acknowledged and gradually replaced by understanding.

Similar approaches can be seen globally, where structured dialogues have fostered peace in divided regions. In Northern Ireland, for example, community-led initiatives brought together Protestant and Catholic groups to address sectarian tensions. These dialogues, often held in neutral locations like community halls, allowed participants to share their grievances, humanize one another, and collaborate on localized solutions. The success of these initiatives reinforces the idea that neutral spaces, combined with skilled facilitation, can dismantle barriers created by mistrust.

Trust is not restored through grand proclamations but through consistent, small-scale actions that demonstrate sincerity and accountability. Collaborative community projects provide an effective way to rebuild trust, as they require individuals from different backgrounds to work together on shared goals. These initiatives not only address tangible needs but also create opportunities for participants to understand and empathize with one another, fostering a sense of mutual respect.

The recovery efforts following Hurricane Katrina in New Orleans illustrate how collaborative projects can transform relationships in divided communities. While the disaster initially exposed deep racial and economic disparities, recovery initiatives brought together diverse groups to rebuild homes, schools, and neighborhoods. Programs like Habitat for Humanity involved volunteers from various racial, economic, and cultural backgrounds, working side by side to restore communities. These efforts not only addressed critical infrastructure needs but also helped participants forge connections that transcended historical divides, demonstrating the potential of incremental trust-building measures.

On a smaller scale, local initiatives such as community gardens, volunteer tutoring programs, or neighborhood safety projects offer similar opportunities for collaboration. These activities encourage individuals to engage with those they might not otherwise interact with, breaking down stereotypes and fostering a sense of shared responsibility. For example, urban renewal projects in cities like Detroit have brought together residents from different racial and socio-economic backgrounds to revitalize abandoned spaces, creating both tangible improvements and a renewed sense of community.

The persistence of mistrust is not just a barrier to reconciliation—it actively undermines progress and cohesion. When groups fail to trust one another, collaboration becomes impossible, and even the most well-intentioned initiatives are met with skepticism. This dynamic creates a feedback loop, where mistrust fuels division, and division further entrenches mistrust.

For instance, mistrust in political institutions can lead to disengagement from the democratic process, leaving critical decisions in the hands of a smaller, less representative group of voters. Similarly, mistrust in law enforcement perpetuates cycles of violence and fear, making it harder to implement reforms that would benefit both officers and communities. On a societal level, mistrust erodes the fabric of collaboration and understanding, stalling progress on urgent issues like climate change, public health, and economic inequality.

By addressing mistrust through dialogue, incremental action, and systemic reform, societies can create a foundation for reconciliation that benefits everyone. Efforts to rebuild trust must be rooted in transparency, accountability, and a commitment to shared goals. While the process is challenging, the potential rewards—stronger communities, healthier relationships, and a more cohesive society—make it an essential undertaking.

Inadequate Structural Change

Reconciliation efforts often falter when systemic issues such as economic inequality, discriminatory policies, and unequal access to opportunities remain unaddressed. While dialogue and symbolic gestures are important components of reconciliation, they cannot replace the need for substantive structural reforms. Without addressing these foundational inequities, reconciliation risks being superficial and short-lived, leaving underlying grievances unresolved and communities vulnerable to further division.

A major barrier to lasting reconciliation is the failure to pair it with tangible reforms that address the root causes of division and inequality. Symbolic acts, such as public apologies or commemorations, can foster goodwill in the short term but do little to dismantle systemic inequities. Without addressing these deeper issues, reconciliation efforts can come across as performative, leaving affected communities feeling neglected or deceived.

One of the clearest examples of this dynamic is the United States' handling of racial inequality following the civil rights advances of the 1960s. While landmark legislation like the Civil Rights Act and the Voting Rights Act represented significant progress, these gains were not accompanied by robust economic reforms to address the racial wealth gap created by centuries of systemic oppression. Practices like redlining, unequal access to education, and employment discrimination persisted, perpetuating cycles of poverty in marginalized communities. As of 2021, Black families hold only a fraction of the wealth of white families, highlighting the enduring economic disparities that reconciliation efforts have failed to address.

Similarly, in post-conflict nations, reconciliation programs that focus solely on symbolic gestures or truth-telling often neglect the economic and social disparities that fueled conflict in the first place. For instance, in South Africa, the Truth and Reconciliation Commission (TRC) provided a platform for victims and perpetrators of apartheid-era abuses to share their stories. While this process helped to foster dialogue and healing, it did not address the structural inequalities entrenched by apartheid, such as unequal land ownership, poverty, and lack of access to quality education for Black South Africans. These lingering disparities continue to challenge South Africa's progress toward a more equitable society.

To create lasting reconciliation, efforts must be paired with structural reforms that address the root causes of division and inequality. This approach requires a commitment to equitable resource distribution, access to education, healthcare improvements, and meaningful economic opportunities. Without these systemic changes, reconciliation initiatives risk being seen as empty gestures, further eroding trust between communities and institutions.

One of the most effective ways to address systemic inequality is through equitable resource distribution. This includes investing in underserved communities to provide access to quality education, healthcare, and economic opportunities. For example, countries that have successfully reduced disparities often implement targeted funding for schools in low-income areas, ensuring that every child has access to the tools they need to succeed. Similarly, investments in affordable housing and job training programs can help bridge economic gaps, fostering a sense of shared opportunity and progress. Research demonstrates that these targeted efforts not only improve individual outcomes but also contribute to broader societal benefits, such as reduced crime rates and increased economic productivity.

Education is a cornerstone of systemic reform. By ensuring equitable access to education, societies can empower individuals to overcome systemic barriers and contribute to reconciliation efforts. Initiatives like school desegregation and increased funding for historically underfunded schools in the U.S. have made strides in addressing educational disparities, but much work remains to be done. Policies that promote free or affordable higher education and vocational training can provide marginalized communities with pathways to upward mobility, creating the conditions for sustainable reconciliation.

Healthcare is another critical area for structural reform.

Disparities in healthcare access and outcomes disproportionately affect marginalized communities, perpetuating cycles of inequality. Implementing universal healthcare systems, as seen in countries like Finland, can ensure that all citizens have access to the medical care they need, regardless of their socioeconomic status. Improved healthcare access not only addresses immediate needs but also fosters trust in institutions and demonstrates a commitment to equity.

For reconciliation initiatives to succeed, they must be designed with input from the communities they aim to serve. Too often, reconciliation programs are imposed from the top down, failing to address the specific needs and concerns of affected populations. By involving communities in the planning and implementation of reconciliation efforts, policymakers can ensure that these programs are relevant, inclusive, and effective.

The failure to address systemic issues is one of the most significant barriers to meaningful reconciliation. Without structural reforms, efforts to foster dialogue and healing remain incomplete, leaving the root causes of division unaddressed. Reconciliation is not just about symbolic gestures or public apologies—it must involve dismantling the systems and structures that perpetuate inequality and exclusion. Whether it's economic disparities, unequal access to education, or systemic discrimination, these foundational issues must be confronted to create the conditions for lasting unity and progress. A failure to do so risks reducing reconciliation to a superficial process that fails to inspire meaningful change.

True reconciliation demands a holistic approach that combines dialogue, education, and policy reform. Dialogue can foster understanding and empathy, but it cannot succeed without the support of substantive changes that address systemic barriers. For example, equitable resource distribution in areas such as healthcare, housing, and education ensures that reconciliation extends beyond words to tangible improvements in people's lives. Policies that target underserved communities and close opportunity gaps are essential for fostering trust and creating a society where reconciliation is more than a fleeting aspiration.

These systemic reforms are not merely about correcting injustices—they are about building a society where every individual has the tools and opportunities to thrive.

This integration of systemic reform with reconciliation efforts also requires the involvement of institutions at every level. Governments must implement policies that address structural inequities, corporations must prioritize ethical practices that promote equity, and community organizations must champion grassroots initiatives that empower marginalized groups. Only through such widespread commitment can reconciliation become a transformative process. When societies address the systems that perpetuate inequality, they demonstrate that reconciliation is not just about healing the wounds of the past but also about forging a future rooted in justice and inclusion. The process will require patience and persistence, but its impact will ripple across generations.

As this chapter concludes, it is clear that tackling the structural causes of division is not optional; it is essential for meaningful reconciliation. By pairing dialogue with substantive reforms, societies can create a foundation for sustainable unity. In the chapters to come, we will explore actionable steps that individuals, communities, and institutions can take to ensure reconciliation is not a temporary solution but a lasting transformation. Through collective action, empathy, and a shared commitment to dismantling systemic barriers, we can build a future where reconciliation is not only possible but becomes the cornerstone of a more equitable and inclusive society.

Social Investment: Education

Education lies at the heart of nearly every societal debate, and for good reason. Whether addressing economic inequality, racial disparities, or technological advancement, the conversation often circles back to education. It is both the root of many challenges and the key to unlocking transformative solutions. Education equips individuals with the tools to navigate a rapidly changing world, empowers communities to thrive, and drives progress on a national and global scale. It is not merely an individual endeavor but a public good that serves as the backbone of equitable, prosperous societies.

Despite this universal recognition of its importance, education systems worldwide, and particularly in the United States, remain deeply flawed. Disparities in access to quality education perpetuate cycles of inequality, limiting opportunities for millions and stunting societal progress. Wealthier districts benefit from well-funded schools with cutting-edge resources, while low-income communities struggle to provide students with basic needs. The unequal distribution of educational opportunities is not just an injustice—it is a profound failure to invest in the future.

This brings us back to the question we have asked repeatedly throughout history: how can education serve as the great equalizer it is often proclaimed to be? From debates over desegregation in the mid-20th century to today's battles over school funding and curriculum reform, the question of how to achieve equitable education remains unresolved. While strides have been made, such as the expansion of public education and programs like Head Start, progress has often been piecemeal and insufficient. The persistent gaps in achievement, access, and opportunity demand renewed focus and bold action.

At its core, education is a shared responsibility. While individuals are the direct beneficiaries of education, its ripple effects extend far beyond personal success. Communities with strong educational systems experience lower crime rates, higher economic productivity, and greater civic engagement. Conversely, communities deprived of quality education face entrenched poverty, social unrest, and diminished prospects for future generations. This interconnectedness makes education a societal obligation, not just an individual pursuit.

Historically, the United States has recognized education's transformative power. The establishment of public schooling in the 19th century, the passage of the G.I. Bill after World War II, and the desegregation efforts of the Civil Rights Movement all reflected an understanding that education is key to societal progress. However, each of these milestones also exposed the inequities embedded within the system. Public schools in affluent neighborhoods flourished while those in underfunded districts languished. The promise of the G.I. Bill was often inaccessible to Black veterans due to discriminatory practices. Even desegregation, while a landmark victory, faced relentless resistance and left enduring inequalities in its wake.

Today, the challenges in education have evolved but remain rooted in the same fundamental issues of equity and access. Rising tuition costs and the crushing weight of student loan debt have turned higher education into a privilege rather than a right for many. The digital divide has widened educational disparities, as students in underserved areas struggle to access the technology needed to succeed in modern classrooms. These barriers underscore a painful truth: education, in its current form, often reinforces inequality rather than dismantling it.

The persistence of these challenges forces us to confront the foundational question anew: what would it take to create an education system that truly levels the playing field? The answer lies in reimagining education as a social investment. This perspective shifts the focus from short-term costs to long-term benefits, recognizing that equitable education systems yield returns far beyond the classroom. Investing in education means investing in innovation, economic growth, and social stability. It is a commitment to nurturing talent, fostering inclusion, and ensuring that every individual has the opportunity to reach their full potential.

To do this, we must address the structural inequities that plague the system. Funding models that rely heavily on local property taxes perpetuate disparities, as wealthier communities can allocate more resources to their schools while low-income areas are left behind. Reforming these funding mechanisms is essential to ensuring that every child, regardless of their zip code, has access to quality education. Similarly, policies that expand access to early childhood education, reduce class sizes, and support teacher training are critical to closing the achievement gap.

In addition to systemic reforms, we must also embrace innovation. Technology, when leveraged effectively, has the potential to bridge educational divides. Online learning platforms, digital resources, and virtual classrooms can bring high-quality education to underserved communities, providing students with tools to thrive in a knowledge-based economy. However, this requires addressing the digital divide, ensuring that every student has access to reliable internet and modern devices. Technology is not a cure-all, but it can be a powerful tool for leveling the playing field.

Another essential component of reimagining education is expanding the definition of success. Traditional metrics like standardized test scores and graduation rates, while important, do not capture the full range of skills and competencies needed in the 21st century. Education systems must prioritize critical thinking, creativity, emotional intelligence, and civic engagement, equipping students to tackle complex challenges and contribute meaningfully to society. This broader vision of education acknowledges that success is not one-size-fits-all and embraces the diversity of talents and aspirations within each classroom.

As we begin this chapter, it's clear that the role of education in shaping our future has never been more critical. In a world increasingly driven by innovation, interconnected economies, and pressing social challenges, the need for a comprehensive and equitable education system is undeniable. This chapter will unpack the complexities of treating education as a true societal investment, exploring how we can address disparities, broaden access, and redefine its potential.

Barriers to Equal Education Access

One of the most glaring issues in American education is the reliance on local property taxes to fund public schools. This system inherently favors affluent neighborhoods, where higher property values generate more revenue for schools. In contrast, schools in lower-income areas—both urban and rural—struggle with inadequate funding, leading to overcrowded classrooms, outdated materials, and insufficient resources for students with special needs.

For example, a 2019 report from EdBuild highlighted that predominantly White school districts received $23 billion more in funding than districts serving predominantly non-White students, despite serving a similar number of students. This inequity directly impacts educational outcomes, as well-funded schools can afford experienced teachers, advanced coursework, and extracurricular activities that enrich learning. Conversely, underfunded schools often lack basic infrastructure, let alone the resources needed to compete in a rapidly changing global economy.

The effects of funding disparities in education are far-reaching, influencing not only academic outcomes but also the broader well-being of students. Schools with limited budgets often lack the resources to provide essential services such as mental health counseling and social-emotional support. For many students, these services are critical to navigating challenges both inside and outside the classroom, including stress, trauma, and family instability. Without access to mental health professionals or trained counselors, students in underfunded schools are left to manage these challenges on their own, which can negatively impact their academic performance, self-esteem, and long-term prospects.

Beyond mental health, these funding gaps deprive students of opportunities for personal growth through extracurricular activities, such as sports teams, music programs, and academic clubs. Extracurriculars are more than just optional pastimes— they are vital for building teamwork, leadership, and time-management skills. They also serve as pathways for college scholarships and career opportunities, particularly for students from low-income backgrounds. When schools lack the funding to maintain these programs, students lose access to experiences that could shape their futures in meaningful ways. In contrast, well-funded schools often offer a rich array of extracurricular options, further widening the gap between advantaged and disadvantaged students.

This lack of holistic support creates a compounding effect. Students in underfunded districts enter the workforce or higher education with fewer skills, lower confidence, and reduced networks compared to their peers in well-funded schools. Over time, this exacerbates cycles of poverty and inequality, limiting social mobility for entire communities. Addressing these disparities requires a shift in how educational resources are allocated, prioritizing equity to ensure that all students— regardless of where they live—receive the support they need to thrive academically, emotionally, and socially. Only by recognizing the importance of holistic student development can we begin to create a more equitable education system.

Although legal segregation was abolished decades ago, American schools remain deeply divided along racial and socioeconomic lines. According to a 2022 report by the Civil Rights Project at UCLA, more than half of all Black and Hispanic students attend schools where at least 75% of the student body is non-White, and these schools are often underfunded compared to predominantly White schools. This de facto segregation perpetuates disparities in educational opportunities, as students in segregated schools frequently face lower expectations, fewer advanced placement courses, and less access to college preparatory resources.

School segregation not only limits educational opportunities but also exacerbates social divides. Students in segregated schools are less likely to interact with peers from different racial or socioeconomic backgrounds, missing opportunities to build understanding and empathy. These divides extend into adulthood, reinforcing societal polarization and hindering collective progress.

While much attention is given to urban education challenges, rural schools face unique barriers that are often overlooked. Rural districts frequently lack the tax base to fund schools adequately, leaving them with fewer resources than their urban and suburban counterparts. These schools struggle to attract and retain qualified teachers due to lower salaries, geographic isolation, and limited professional development opportunities.

Moreover, rural schools often lack access to advanced coursework, extracurricular activities, and college counseling services, limiting students' post-graduation options. The digital divide is particularly pronounced in rural areas, where many students lack reliable internet access, making it difficult to participate in online learning or complete assignments that require digital resources. These challenges disproportionately affect poor White and Indigenous communities, perpetuating cycles of poverty and educational inequity.

In today's increasingly digital world, access to technology is essential for academic success. Yet, millions of students across the United States lack the devices and internet access needed to fully participate in modern education. A 2020 report from Common Sense Media estimated that 15 to 16 million K-12 students live in households without adequate internet connectivity, a disparity exacerbated during the COVID-19 pandemic when schools shifted to online learning.

This digital divide disproportionately impacts students in low-income, rural, and urban communities, where families may struggle to afford devices or broadband services. Without access to technology, students face significant challenges in completing assignments, conducting research, and developing digital literacy skills that are crucial for success in higher education and the workforce.

The digital divide is not just a technological issue—it is a civil rights issue. Inadequate access to technology creates a two-tiered education system where students from marginalized communities are systematically excluded from opportunities to thrive in a technology-driven world. Addressing this divide requires both immediate solutions, such as providing devices and internet subsidies, and long-term investments in infrastructure to ensure equitable access for all students.

The barriers to quality education do not exist in isolation; they intersect and disproportionately affect marginalized communities, including poor White, Black, and Hispanic Americans. For example, a low-income Black student in an urban district may face underfunded schools, school segregation, and limited access to technology. Similarly, a poor White student in a rural area may encounter underfunded schools, a lack of advanced coursework, and unreliable internet access. While the specific challenges may vary, the cumulative effect is the same: diminished opportunities and a perpetuation of generational inequality.

These disparities also have far-reaching societal consequences. Students who are denied access to quality education are less likely to achieve economic stability, leading to higher rates of unemployment, underemployment, and reliance on public assistance. This not only affects individual lives but also places a strain on social safety nets and limits the nation's overall economic growth.

The barriers to quality education do not exist in isolation; they are interconnected and disproportionately affect marginalized communities, including poor White, Black, and Hispanic Americans. A low-income Black student in an urban district may face a combination of underfunded schools, the lingering effects of segregation, and limited access to the technology necessary for modern learning. Similarly, a poor White student in a rural area may grapple with underfunded schools, a lack of advanced coursework or extracurricular opportunities, and unreliable internet access. These issues may manifest differently depending on geography and demographics, but the cumulative result is the same: diminished opportunities, generational inequality, and a loss of potential that affects society as a whole.

What we lose in these disparities is more than just individual success stories; it is the potential for societal breakthroughs. Without equitable access to education, countless students who could become scientists, engineers, educators, or artists are denied the opportunity to contribute their talents. Consider the challenges the world faces today—climate change, healthcare disparities, technological innovation, and societal polarization. The solutions to these problems may well lie in the untapped minds of students who are never given the tools to realize their potential. A nation that fails to educate all its citizens equitably limits its ability to innovate, compete globally, and build a sustainable future. For instance, a student with an innate aptitude for science or technology in a poorly funded school may never gain access to advanced STEM programs, cutting off their path to contributing to critical fields like cancer research or renewable energy development.

The societal costs extend even further. Students who are denied access to quality education are less likely to achieve economic stability, leading to higher rates of unemployment, underemployment, and reliance on public assistance. This not only impacts individual lives but also places a strain on already overburdened social safety nets, while simultaneously reducing the nation's tax base and economic productivity. According to numerous studies, nations with equitable education systems experience greater economic mobility and higher rates of innovation, underscoring the link between educational opportunity and a thriving society. When education fails to reach marginalized communities, it creates a ripple effect of lost potential, limited economic growth, and entrenched inequality that harms everyone, not just those directly affected.

To overcome these barriers, we must view education as a collective responsibility, one that requires a commitment to equity and access. Reforming outdated funding structures, expanding connectivity in underserved areas, and fostering diversity within classrooms are not just policies—they are steps toward creating a more inclusive and thriving society. These changes demand action from all levels, from local communities to national leaders, ensuring that every child has the resources they need to succeed.

True educational progress is about more than closing gaps; it's about creating spaces where students from every background can excel, innovate, and contribute meaningfully to the world. Breaking free from generational cycles of disparity is a challenge, but it's also an opportunity to reimagine what education can achieve when barriers are removed. In this effort, every investment made in schools, teachers, and students serves as an investment in the future of society itself.

What happens when education isn't just a response to inequality but a catalyst for transformation? By addressing these challenges with intention and urgency, we can lay the groundwork for an education system that not only levels the playing field but redefines what is possible. It's in this vision that the true power of education begins to emerge.

Education as an Engine for Equity

Universal pre-kindergarten (pre-K) programs exemplify how early educational interventions can transform individual lives and entire communities. Research consistently shows that the early years of a child's life are critical for brain development and learning, making access to quality early education particularly impactful. Universal pre-K ensures that all children, regardless of socioeconomic background, have access to these formative opportunities.

In the United States, Oklahoma stands out as a pioneer in this area. Since implementing universal pre-K in 1998, the state has reported significant improvements in literacy, numeracy, and social-emotional skills among participants. These gains are especially pronounced for children from low-income families, who often face developmental delays due to a lack of resources and stimulation at home. By addressing these disparities early, universal pre-K helps level the playing field, ensuring that all children begin their educational journey with a strong foundation.

The ripple effects of universal pre-K extend far beyond the classroom. Studies have shown that children who attend pre-K are more likely to graduate from high school, pursue higher education, and secure stable employment. Additionally, early childhood education programs have been linked to reductions in crime rates and reliance on public assistance later in life. These outcomes demonstrate that investing in pre-K is not just an investment in individual children—it is an investment in the future economic and social well-being of entire communities.

Community colleges play a crucial role in expanding access to higher education and addressing the skills gap in the modern workforce. Programs like Tennessee Promise, which offers tuition-free community college to high school graduates, have been game-changers for students who might otherwise struggle to afford postsecondary education. These programs provide an entry point to higher education and create pathways to careers that require specialized training or certifications.

The impact of community colleges extends beyond individual students to the broader economy. Many industries face a growing skills gap, struggling to find workers with the technical expertise required to fill high-demand roles. Community colleges are uniquely positioned to bridge this gap by offering affordable, targeted training in areas such as healthcare, information technology, and advanced manufacturing. In doing so, they not only empower students to secure higher-paying jobs but also help businesses remain competitive in a global economy.

Moreover, community colleges often serve as engines of local economic development. Graduates tend to remain in their communities, contributing to the local economy through increased spending and tax revenues. For example, a report by the American Association of Community Colleges found that community colleges contribute nearly $800 billion annually to the U.S. economy. This underscores the profound impact that accessible higher education can have on individual and collective prosperity.

These examples illustrate the profound societal benefits of investing in education at all levels. Universal pre-K programs lay the foundation for lifelong success, equipping children with the skills they need to thrive academically and socially while reducing societal costs related to crime and public assistance. Similarly, community colleges serve as vital gateways to economic mobility, empowering individuals to gain the training and credentials needed for in-demand careers. These institutions are not just pathways to personal achievement—they are pillars of community and economic resilience.

Education's impact extends far beyond academics and the workforce—it also plays a critical role in reducing crime rates and improving public health outcomes. Research consistently shows a strong correlation between educational attainment and lower crime rates. Communities with higher levels of education experience reduced rates of violent crime, property crime, and incarceration. This is not merely coincidental; education provides individuals with greater opportunities for economic stability, reducing the desperation that often leads to criminal behavior.

Additionally, education equips individuals with critical thinking skills and a greater awareness of the consequences of their actions, fostering a sense of personal responsibility and civic engagement. Programs like prison education initiatives further underscore this connection. Inmates who participate in educational programs while incarcerated are significantly less likely to reoffend upon release, demonstrating the rehabilitative power of education in breaking cycles of crime and recidivism.

Education also contributes to better health outcomes, both at the individual and societal levels. Higher levels of education are associated with longer life expectancy, lower rates of chronic diseases, and improved mental health. Educated individuals are more likely to make informed decisions about their health, access preventive care, and advocate for themselves within the healthcare system. Moreover, communities with higher levels of education tend to have better access to healthcare facilities and services, creating a ripple effect that benefits entire populations.

Education is the engine that drives innovation, creativity, and economic growth. By providing individuals with the knowledge and skills needed to tackle complex challenges, education lays the groundwork for advancements in science, technology, medicine, and the arts. History offers countless examples of how education has fueled progress, from the scientific breakthroughs of the Enlightenment to the technological revolution of the 20th century.

In today's rapidly evolving global economy, the demand for skilled workers continues to grow. Equitable education ensures that no talent goes untapped, allowing individuals from all backgrounds to contribute to innovation and progress. Programs that promote STEM (science, technology, engineering, and math) education, for example, have been instrumental in preparing students for careers in high-demand fields. By investing in these programs, societies can address critical challenges such as climate change, public health crises, and infrastructure development.

The economic benefits of education are also far-reaching. According to the World Bank, each additional year of schooling can increase an individual's earnings by an average of 8-10%. At the national level, countries with higher levels of education experience faster economic growth, greater productivity, and reduced income inequality. These benefits extend to all members of society, creating a virtuous cycle of prosperity and stability.

Equitable education also plays a vital role in reducing societal polarization. In deeply divided societies, access to quality education can serve as a unifying force, fostering mutual understanding and respect. Schools are often the first places where individuals from diverse backgrounds interact, providing opportunities to break down stereotypes and build connections. By promoting inclusive curricula that celebrate diversity and encourage critical thinking, education can help bridge cultural and ideological divides.

Programs that emphasize civic education and media literacy

are particularly important in combating polarization. Civic education equips students with the tools to engage in constructive dialogue, understand different perspectives, and participate actively in democratic processes. Media literacy, on the other hand, helps individuals navigate the complex landscape of information in the digital age, reducing the influence of misinformation and fostering informed decision-making.

When education prioritizes equity and inclusivity, it sends a powerful message: every individual has value, and every voice matters. This message is essential in countering the divisive narratives that fuel polarization and mistrust. By creating spaces for dialogue and collaboration, education can pave the way for a more cohesive and united society.

To fully realize education's potential as an engine for equity, significant systemic changes are needed. Policymakers must address the root causes of educational disparities, including funding inequities, segregation, and access to technology. This requires bold investments in underserved communities, targeted support for marginalized populations, and reforms that prioritize inclusivity and diversity.

Equally important is the need to shift societal attitudes toward education. Education must be seen not as a commodity but as a public good that benefits everyone. This means fostering a culture that values lifelong learning, supports educators, and prioritizes the needs of students over bureaucratic or political interests.

Policy Solutions for Equitable Education

The disparities in education access and quality in the United States are the result of systemic inequities that demand bold, targeted policy responses. Education, often regarded as the great equalizer, must be treated as a public good, with reforms focused on building a foundation of fairness and opportunity. Addressing these disparities is not just a matter of justice—it is a strategic investment in the nation's economic, social, and cultural future. Transforming the education system into a more equitable and effective engine for progress requires systemic changes that prioritize underserved communities and ensure access to quality education for all.

At the heart of educational equity is the need to reform the current system of school funding. Tying public school budgets to local property taxes entrenches vast disparities between affluent and low-income districts. Wealthier areas benefit from schools with modern facilities, smaller class sizes, and extensive extracurricular opportunities, while less affluent districts face overcrowding, outdated materials, and underpaid staff. Moving toward a model of equitable funding would address these gaps by ensuring that resources are distributed based on student needs rather than local wealth. This approach would not only reduce immediate disparities but also foster long-term economic growth by empowering underserved communities.

Universal early childhood education is another powerful tool for addressing educational inequity. Early childhood programs level the playing field for young learners, providing them with foundational cognitive and social-emotional skills essential for lifelong success. National implementation of such programs would reduce achievement gaps, increase graduation rates, and enhance workforce readiness, delivering long-term societal benefits by addressing disparities at the earliest stages of development.

Access to higher education also remains a critical component of educational equity. Rising tuition costs create significant barriers, particularly for first-generation college students and those from lower-income families. Expanding financial assistance and tuition-free programs would enable individuals to gain valuable skills and contribute to the economy. These initiatives would also address workforce shortages in high-demand industries while fostering social mobility and empowering individuals to achieve their potential.

The growing digital divide presents another significant challenge to educational equity. Students in rural areas and low-income urban communities often lack access to the internet or necessary devices, limiting their ability to participate in modern education. Bridging this divide requires expanding broadband infrastructure, subsidizing internet access for low-income families, and equipping schools with up-to-date technology. Addressing these gaps is critical to ensuring that all students can fully engage with the increasingly digital nature of education.

No reform can succeed without supporting educators, who are the foundation of the education system. Many teachers face low pay, limited resources, and inadequate professional development opportunities, especially in underfunded schools. Policymakers must prioritize teacher training and support programs to ensure that all classrooms are led by highly qualified educators. Empowering teachers with competitive salaries and professional development opportunities equips them to meet the diverse needs of their students and improves outcomes across the board.

Segregation and lack of diversity in schools continue to undermine educational equity. Schools with homogenous student bodies often lack the range of perspectives necessary for a well-rounded education. Promoting inclusion through enrollment strategies and creating curricula that reflect the diverse histories and contributions of all groups can foster a sense of belonging and mutual understanding, enriching the educational experience for all students.

Accountability and local involvement are critical to ensuring that education reform delivers meaningful results. Metrics for evaluating success should include not only academic achievements but also measures like student well-being and community engagement. Giving parents, teachers, and students a voice in shaping policies ensures that reforms address local needs and foster trust in the system. This community-driven approach builds shared responsibility and strengthens the foundation for lasting educational improvements.

Education has the power to be a transformative force for equity and progress, but realizing its full potential requires systemic change. Addressing disparities in funding, access, and quality is a strategic investment in the nation's future. Through bold reforms, policymakers can create an inclusive education system that serves as a catalyst for opportunity and advancement for all. Equitable education is not just a moral imperative—it is a practical necessity for building a society that thrives economically, socially, and culturally for generations to come.

Social Investment: Diversity Investment

Diversity investment is not merely a moral imperative—it is a strategic necessity for creating equitable, innovative, and resilient societies. At its core, diversity investment involves the intentional cultivation of inclusion and equity across all sectors of society, including workplaces, educational institutions, and community spaces. It requires a commitment to addressing systemic barriers, dismantling biases, and creating environments where individuals from all backgrounds can thrive. This chapter examines diversity as a critical driver of innovation, economic growth, and social cohesion, setting the stage for understanding its transformative potential.

Diversity investment goes beyond token gestures or surface-level initiatives. It entails meaningful efforts to ensure that all individuals—regardless of race, gender, socioeconomic status, religion, sexual orientation, or ability—have access to opportunities and the tools they need to succeed. Studies consistently demonstrate that diversity drives innovation. Teams that include individuals with diverse perspectives are better equipped to solve complex problems, generate creative solutions, and adapt to rapidly changing environments. In the workplace, companies with diverse leadership are more likely to outperform their peers in profitability and productivity, underscoring the tangible benefits of inclusion.

From an economic perspective, diversity is a powerful engine for growth. By tapping into the talents and contributions of all segments of society, nations can expand their economic potential and foster resilience in the face of global competition. Research shows that inclusive economies tend to be more dynamic, with higher levels of entrepreneurship and innovation. Investing in diversity is not just about fairness—it is about maximizing the collective strengths of society and creating pathways for sustainable progress.

Despite its clear benefits, achieving true diversity and inclusion remains a challenge due to systemic barriers and deeply entrenched biases. Marginalized groups often face significant hurdles that limit their access to education, employment, and leadership opportunities. For example, women and racial minorities are underrepresented in senior management and STEM fields, even as these sectors drive much of today's economic growth. These disparities are not merely the result of individual prejudice; they are reinforced by structural inequities, such as unequal access to quality education, wage gaps, and discriminatory hiring practices.

Educational disparities play a central role in perpetuating these inequities. Marginalized communities often lack access to high-quality schools, advanced coursework, and mentorship opportunities, which limits their ability to compete in the labor market. Similarly, workplace environments that fail to prioritize diversity and equity create cultures of exclusion, where marginalized employees feel undervalued or unsupported as touched upon in the many chapters before this one. These challenges are further compounded by unconscious biases, which can influence decisions ranging from hiring to promotions.

Addressing these systemic barriers requires intentionality. It demands policy changes, cultural shifts, and a willingness to confront uncomfortable truths about the structures that perpetuate inequality. Diversity investment is not about charity or quotas—it is about building systems that work for everyone, ensuring that talent and potential are not wasted due to prejudice or exclusion.

The ripple effects of diversity investment extend far beyond the workplace or individual sectors. At a societal level, diversity fosters social cohesion by encouraging cross-cultural understanding and reducing prejudice. When individuals from different backgrounds have the opportunity to interact, collaborate, and share experiences, they are more likely to develop empathy and mutual respect. This, in turn, strengthens the social fabric, reducing polarization and fostering unity.

Educational settings provide a clear example of this dynamic. Diverse classrooms expose students to a wide range of perspectives, helping them develop critical thinking skills and cultural competence. These qualities are essential for success in an increasingly interconnected world. Similarly, communities that embrace diversity tend to be more vibrant and resilient, benefiting from the unique contributions and strengths of their members.

Diversity investment also has the potential to address pressing societal challenges. For example, diverse research teams are more likely to approach problems from multiple angles, leading to breakthroughs in areas like medicine, technology, and environmental sustainability. By including voices that have historically been excluded, societies can unlock new ideas and solutions that benefit everyone.

As this chapter will explore, diversity investment is not just a responsibility for governments or corporations—it is a collective endeavor that requires engagement from individuals, communities, and institutions. Everyone has a role to play in creating a more inclusive and equitable society, whether by advocating for policy changes, fostering inclusive practices in the workplace, or challenging biases in everyday interactions.

The benefits of diversity investment are not limited to marginalized groups; they extend to society as a whole. Inclusive workplaces are more innovative, schools with diverse student bodies produce better outcomes, and communities that prioritize equity experience greater cohesion and resilience. By framing diversity as a shared goal, we can move beyond zero-sum thinking and recognize that equity for one group enhances opportunities for all.

This chapter will delve deeper into the systemic barriers that hinder diversity, as well as the transformative power of inclusion. It will highlight real-world examples of successful diversity investments and explore actionable strategies for creating more inclusive systems. By understanding diversity as both a moral and practical imperative, we can harness its potential to drive progress, innovation, and social cohesion.

The Economic Case for Diversity

Research consistently shows that diverse teams outperform homogeneous ones, particularly in areas requiring creativity, problem-solving, and innovation. This advantage stems from the varied perspectives and experiences that team members bring to the table. Diverse groups approach challenges from multiple angles, identifying solutions that might be overlooked in less inclusive settings. For example, studies have found that gender-diverse companies are 25% more likely to achieve above-average profitability, while companies with ethnic diversity in leadership are 36% more likely to outperform their peers.

Diverse teams also excel in addressing complex, interdisciplinary problems. Whether in medicine, technology, or environmental sustainability, teams with members from different cultural, professional, and academic backgrounds are better equipped to devise groundbreaking solutions. In medicine, for instance, diverse research teams have contributed to advances in personalized treatments by incorporating broader demographic data in their studies. Similarly, technology firms with inclusive teams often develop products that appeal to wider audiences, increasing market share and profitability.

Despite these proven advantages, many organizations struggle to fully embrace diversity in their operations. Structural biases, limited access to leadership opportunities for underrepresented groups, and a lack of accountability often hinder progress. Addressing these barriers is not just a matter of fairness—it is a necessary step toward ensuring that organizations remain competitive in a rapidly evolving global economy.

Representation matters, particularly in leadership. When decision-makers reflect the diversity of their employees, customers, and stakeholders, organizations are better positioned to create inclusive policies and products. Diverse leadership fosters a culture of equity, where voices from all backgrounds are heard and valued. This, in turn, leads to more effective decision-making and increased organizational agility.

Leaders from underrepresented groups bring unique insights into market trends, customer preferences, and employee engagement. Their presence also sends a powerful message to marginalized communities, demonstrating that opportunities for advancement are available to everyone. In industries like technology and finance, where women and minorities remain underrepresented in leadership roles, greater diversity can catalyze broader cultural shifts, encouraging more inclusive hiring and promotion practices across the board.

The economic implications of diverse leadership are far-reaching. Companies with inclusive leadership teams are more likely to attract top talent, retain employees, and enhance customer loyalty. This logical allows diverse boards of directors to make more balanced decisions, reducing risks and increasing long-term profitability. This alignment of equity and efficiency underscores why diversity investment is both a social responsibility and a strategic advantage.

Diversity investment has the potential to address systemic income inequality, one of the most pressing economic challenges of our time. Marginalized groups—whether defined by race, gender, or socioeconomic status—often face barriers to entry in high-paying industries and leadership positions. By actively dismantling these barriers and creating pathways for inclusion, businesses and governments can help reduce wage gaps and promote upward mobility.

Workforce inclusion programs, such as targeted recruitment initiatives and mentorship opportunities, can significantly expand access to high-growth fields like STEM (science, technology, engineering, and mathematics). Providing scholarships, apprenticeships, and career training for underrepresented groups ensures that individuals from all backgrounds have the tools they need to succeed. This not only benefits those individuals but also strengthens the broader economy by increasing workforce participation and productivity.

When marginalized groups are included in the workforce, their contributions have a multiplier effect. Increased earnings lead to greater consumer spending, higher tax revenues, and reduced reliance on social safety nets. For example, the U.S. economy could gain an additional $8 trillion by 2025 through closing the racial wealth gap. Similarly, achieving gender parity in the workforce could boost global GDP by $12 trillion. These figures highlight the immense economic potential of diversity investment, reinforcing its importance as a national and global priority.

In an increasingly interconnected world, businesses that embrace diversity are better equipped to serve global markets. Inclusive companies understand the needs and preferences of diverse customer bases, allowing them to develop products and services that resonate across cultures and demographics. For example, beauty brands that offer products catering to a range of skin tones or technology companies that design accessible interfaces for people with disabilities demonstrate how inclusivity drives market innovation.

Diversity also fosters resilience in times of crisis. Organizations with diverse teams are more adaptable and better able to navigate uncertainty, whether responding to economic downturns, technological disruptions, or shifting consumer demands. By incorporating a wide range of perspectives, these companies are more likely to identify opportunities and mitigate risks, ensuring long-term success.

The cultural and economic benefits of diversity extend beyond individual organizations. Communities that embrace inclusion are more cohesive, innovative, and prosperous. This synergy between diversity and economic growth underscores the need for intentional investment in equity, not just as a moral imperative but as a competitive advantage in a rapidly changing world.

While the benefits of diversity are well-documented, achieving meaningful inclusion remains a challenge. Many organizations lack the infrastructure, accountability, or cultural readiness to implement effective diversity initiatives. Implicit biases, structural inequalities, and limited access to educational or professional opportunities often hinder progress, particularly for marginalized groups.

Moreover, resistance to change within institutions can stymie efforts to create more inclusive workplaces. Some view diversity initiatives as symbolic gestures rather than substantive strategies for economic growth, while others fear that inclusion efforts may threaten existing power structures. Overcoming these challenges requires sustained commitment, leadership buy-in, and measurable goals to ensure that diversity investment translates into tangible outcomes.

Overcoming Systemic Barriers to Diversity

Systemic barriers to diversity are deeply embedded in our societal structures, creating challenges that extend far beyond individual biases. These obstacles, whether overt or subtle, limit access to education, professional networks, and leadership opportunities for marginalized groups, perpetuating cycles of exclusion and inequality. Overcoming these systemic challenges requires intentional, comprehensive efforts to dismantle the foundations of discrimination and create an environment where all individuals have the opportunity to thrive.

One pervasive barrier is workplace discrimination, which continues to undermine diversity efforts despite progress in other areas. Studies have shown that resumes with names perceived as "ethnic" are less likely to receive callbacks, regardless of qualifications. This implicit bias not only narrows opportunities for talented individuals but also reinforces stereotypes that stifle inclusion. Additionally, workplace environments often fail to support diverse employees fully. Many organizations lack clear paths for advancement or fail to address the microaggressions that marginalized workers endure daily. These conditions create a culture of exclusion, where individuals feel undervalued and unsupported, ultimately limiting their ability to contribute effectively.

Education inequities further compound systemic exclusion, as marginalized communities frequently face limited access to high-quality schools, advanced coursework, and mentorship opportunities. These disparities create significant barriers to entry into competitive industries, particularly in STEM fields, where representation for women and people of color remains disproportionately low. The lack of foundational resources in early education ripples through the workforce, excluding talented individuals from key roles that drive economic and technological progress. Addressing these disparities is critical for creating an equitable pipeline of talent, which will benefit both individuals and society as a whole.

Intersectionality adds another layer of complexity to the challenges faced by marginalized groups. Women of color, for instance, navigate the dual barriers of gender and racial discrimination, often finding themselves excluded from initiatives that address only one aspect of their identity. Similarly, LGBTQ+ individuals from low-income or minority backgrounds face unique obstacles that cannot be resolved through generalized diversity policies. These overlapping identities highlight the need for a nuanced approach to diversity investment—one that considers the unique experiences of individuals at the intersection of multiple marginalized groups and addresses their specific needs.

The consequences of systemic exclusion are far-reaching, affecting not only individuals but also organizations and society at large. Homogeneous leadership and decision-making bodies are more prone to groupthink, limiting innovation and the effectiveness of policies. For example, public policies designed without input from marginalized communities often fail to address their unique needs, exacerbating existing disparities. This exclusion also fosters distrust in institutions, as those who are excluded see little reflection of their identities or experiences in positions of power. The resulting alienation undermines social cohesion and makes it difficult to build consensus around solutions to pressing societal challenges.

Cultural shifts within organizations and communities are essential to overcoming these systemic barriers. Companies must go beyond surface-level diversity initiatives and embrace practices that foster genuine inclusion. Blind recruitment processes, transparent promotion criteria, and robust mentorship programs are essential steps in creating equitable opportunities. Organizations must also actively combat biases by fostering inclusive workplace cultures that value diverse perspectives. These efforts not only benefit marginalized employees but also drive innovation and improve organizational performance.

Policy changes are equally important in addressing systemic barriers to diversity. Governments must enforce anti-discrimination laws, invest in underfunded schools, and provide resources for marginalized communities to access higher education and professional opportunities. These structural reforms are critical for dismantling the systemic inequities that perpetuate exclusion. Furthermore, accountability mechanisms must be established to ensure that diversity initiatives produce tangible outcomes. Metrics such as representation in leadership, pay equity, and employee satisfaction can provide valuable insights into the effectiveness of these efforts.

Despite the challenges, the potential benefits of overcoming systemic barriers to diversity are immense. Diverse teams are more innovative and effective at problem-solving, bringing a range of perspectives that drive breakthroughs in medicine, technology, and sustainability. Inclusive workplaces attract top talent, retain employees, and enhance customer loyalty, contributing to long-term profitability. At a societal level, diversity fosters economic growth, reduces income inequality, and strengthens social cohesion. By addressing systemic barriers, we can unlock the full potential of our collective talent, creating a more equitable and prosperous future for all.

The road to genuine diversity and inclusion is not easy, but it is essential. Overcoming systemic barriers requires a commitment to continuous improvement, as well as the recognition that diversity is not just about representation—it is about creating environments where everyone can thrive. By addressing discrimination, education inequities, and workplace biases, we can create a society that values and benefits from the contributions of all its members. The rewards of such an effort—a more innovative, equitable, and cohesive world—are well worth the investment.

Policy and Organizational Solutions

Investing in diversity is more than a moral imperative—it is a strategic choice that benefits individuals, organizations, and society as a whole. Yet achieving meaningful change requires actionable strategies implemented at multiple levels, from government policy to workplace practices and community initiatives. Targeted efforts can dismantle systemic barriers, foster inclusion, and create a more equitable future.

At the societal level, policies such as affirmative action, diversity quotas, and equal pay initiatives have been instrumental in addressing historical inequalities. Affirmative action programs aim to level the playing field by prioritizing underrepresented groups in education and employment opportunities. While these programs often face criticism and legal challenges, they have significantly increased representation for marginalized communities in fields where they were historically excluded. Expanding and refining these policies can ensure that they continue to provide meaningful opportunities while addressing concerns about fairness and meritocracy.

Diversity quotas can be a contentious topic, but their effectiveness in increasing representation is well-documented. Countries like Norway, which mandates gender quotas for corporate boards, have seen a significant increase in women's representation in leadership positions. While quotas alone cannot eliminate workplace biases, they create visibility for underrepresented groups and pave the way for systemic change. In the U.S., similar approaches could be applied to corporate governance, public sector roles, and higher education admissions, ensuring a more equitable distribution of opportunities.

Equal pay initiatives are another crucial component of diversity investment. The gender pay gap and racial wage disparities persist across industries, limiting economic mobility for marginalized groups. Legislation that mandates pay transparency and penalizes discriminatory practices can help close these gaps. Additionally, tax incentives for companies that achieve pay equity can encourage compliance and foster a culture of fairness. By addressing income inequality, these policies create a foundation for economic inclusion and social cohesion.

Organizations play a pivotal role in advancing diversity through equitable hiring, inclusive cultures, and robust mentorship programs. The hiring process is often the first barrier for underrepresented groups, as implicit biases and traditional recruitment methods favor candidates with privileged backgrounds. Implementing blind recruitment processes, where identifying information like names and educational institutions are removed, can help reduce bias and level the playing field. Additionally, partnerships with minority-serving institutions and outreach programs in underrepresented communities can diversify candidate pools.

Bias training is another critical tool for fostering inclusive workplace environments. These programs, when done effectively, help employees recognize and address their own unconscious biases, creating a culture of awareness and accountability. However, training alone is insufficient without structural changes. Organizations must pair these efforts with clear diversity metrics, transparent promotion criteria, and mechanisms for reporting discrimination. By embedding accountability into workplace culture, companies can ensure that diversity goals translate into tangible outcomes.

Mentorship and sponsorship programs also play a vital role in advancing underrepresented employees. Mentorship provides guidance and support, while sponsorship involves advocating for individuals in decision-making spaces. Studies show that employees with mentors are more likely to receive promotions and leadership opportunities, yet marginalized groups often lack access to these networks. Creating formal mentorship programs that prioritize diversity ensures that all employees have the tools to succeed and advance in their careers.

The impact of diversity investment extends beyond individual organizations to entire communities. Scholarships for underrepresented groups are a powerful way to address educational disparities and foster a diverse pipeline of talent. Programs like the Gates Millennium Scholars initiative, which provides financial support for low-income minority students, have transformed lives and contributed to increased representation in fields like STEM and healthcare. Expanding such programs can create more equitable access to education and opportunities.

Supporting minority-owned businesses is another avenue for promoting diversity and economic inclusion. Entrepreneurs from marginalized backgrounds often face systemic barriers, such as limited access to capital and mentorship. Initiatives like targeted small business loans, grants, and incubator programs can empower these entrepreneurs, creating jobs and fostering innovation in underserved communities. Public and private sector partnerships can amplify these efforts, providing the resources and networks needed for sustained success.

Community engagement initiatives that promote cross-cultural understanding are equally important. Festivals, workshops, and public dialogues that celebrate diversity can help break down stereotypes and foster mutual respect. These events create spaces for people from different backgrounds to connect, learn, and collaborate, building bridges that strengthen the social fabric.

Education and media are two powerful tools for shifting societal attitudes and fostering diversity. Curricula that highlight the contributions of marginalized groups and address historical injustices create a more inclusive narrative that benefits all students. Schools should integrate culturally responsive teaching practices, ensuring that every child feels seen and valued in the classroom.

Media representation also plays a significant role in shaping perceptions. Diverse portrayals in television, film, and advertising challenge stereotypes and normalize inclusion. Companies that prioritize diversity in their creative teams and content not only reflect society more accurately but also appeal to a broader audience. Positive representation can inspire future generations, showing them that success is possible regardless of their background.

Effective diversity investment requires measurable goals and accountability mechanisms. Companies and governments must set clear benchmarks for representation, pay equity, and inclusion, regularly assessing progress through data collection and reporting. Transparency in these efforts builds trust and ensures that initiatives are not merely performative but result in meaningful change.

Organizations can conduct annual diversity audits, examining metrics such as hiring rates, promotion patterns, and employee satisfaction. Governments can track the outcomes of affirmative action programs and equal pay initiatives, ensuring that policies achieve their intended effects. By sharing best practices and learning from successful models, both public and private sector entities can refine their approaches and drive continuous improvement.

Implementing diversity initiatives is not without its challenges. Resistance to change, competing priorities, and limited resources can hinder progress. However, these obstacles can be overcome through strong leadership, collaboration, and a commitment to the long-term benefits of diversity. Engaging stakeholders at all levels—employees, community members, and policymakers—ensures that efforts are inclusive and sustainable.

The opportunities created by diversity investment far outweigh the challenges. Diverse teams are more innovative, organizations with inclusive cultures attract top talent, and equitable communities experience greater social cohesion. By addressing systemic barriers and implementing targeted solutions, we can unlock the full potential of our society, fostering progress and prosperity for all.

Diversity is not just a buzzword—it is a cornerstone of progress and equity. The strategies outlined provide a roadmap for creating a more inclusive society, one where every individual has the opportunity to thrive. From affirmative action policies and workplace practices to community-based initiatives and educational reforms, the solutions are within reach if we commit to implementing them with intention and accountability.

Ending systemic exclusion requires collective effort and a willingness to confront uncomfortable truths. But the rewards— a society that values every voice, an economy that thrives on innovation, and communities that celebrate their differences—are worth the investment. By prioritizing diversity, we create a future that reflects the best of who we are and what we can achieve together. This chapter may conclude here, but the work to build a more inclusive and equitable world continues, requiring each of us to play our part.

Part IV: A Bright, Shared Future

"The best way to predict the future is to create it.."
- Peter Drucker, Unk.

Practical Steps for Individuals

Change, at its core, begins with individuals. While systemic reform and large-scale initiatives are crucial for tackling societal challenges, they are often built on the foundation of countless individual actions. Each choice we make—how we treat others, the causes we support, and the values we uphold—has the potential to ripple outward, creating a broader impact than we might imagine. This chapter focuses on the power of individual action as a catalyst for collective progress, showing that every person, regardless of their circumstances, has a role to play in building a more equitable and united society.

It's easy to feel powerless in the face of massive societal issues like inequality, polarization, and injustice. The scale of these problems can leave us paralyzed, believing that only governments, corporations, or large organizations have the ability to drive change. However, history has shown time and again that significant movements often begin with individuals— ordinary people who decide to act according to their principles. The Civil Rights Movement in the United States, for instance, was not solely the result of legislative efforts but also the culmination of countless individual acts of courage, from Rosa Parks refusing to give up her seat to thousands of citizens participating in sit-ins, marches, and voter registration drives.

The power of individual action lies in its ability to inspire others and create momentum. One person's decision to act can encourage those around them to do the same, gradually building a collective force that becomes impossible to ignore. Whether it's choosing to support local businesses, engaging in conversations about difficult topics, or volunteering in underserved communities, these seemingly small actions can have far-reaching effects when multiplied across society. Change often starts with the simple question: What can I do in my own sphere of influence?

Importantly, individual action is not about perfection or grand gestures. It's about consistency and intention. Nobody can do everything, but everybody can do something. This mindset allows us to focus on what is within our control, rather than being overwhelmed by what isn't. It also emphasizes that meaningful contributions come in many forms, tailored to each person's skills, resources, and circumstances. A teacher might use their platform to promote critical thinking and empathy in the classroom, while a business owner might prioritize hiring practices that foster diversity and inclusion. Both are valuable and necessary forms of individual action.

Individual action also helps to bridge divides, fostering empathy and understanding in ways that large-scale initiatives often cannot. When people take the time to connect on a personal level, they begin to see one another as individuals rather than stereotypes or representatives of opposing groups. This can be as simple as having a conversation with someone who holds different beliefs, listening to their perspective without judgment, and finding common ground. These small acts of connection can soften the edges of polarization, making it easier for communities to work together toward shared goals.

For many, the idea of addressing societal issues through individual action might seem inadequate—like trying to empty an ocean with a spoon. However, the reality is that systems and institutions are made up of individuals. Laws are written and enforced by people. Organizations are run by people. Cultural norms are shaped by people. Every system we interact with is influenced, in some way, by the choices and behaviors of individuals within it. By changing how we act and interact, we can begin to shift the systems themselves.

Another crucial aspect of individual action is its potential to challenge apathy. In a world where it's easy to feel disconnected from issues that don't directly affect us, individual actions remind us of our shared humanity. When someone donates their time or resources to help those in need, it sends a message that every life has value and that we are all responsible for one another's well-being. This sense of responsibility can be contagious, inspiring others to care and act in turn.

It's also important to recognize that individual action doesn't require extraordinary resources. While financial contributions to causes are certainly impactful, they are not the only way to make a difference. Time, energy, and advocacy are equally valuable. Volunteering at a local shelter, mentoring a young person, or even amplifying important messages on social media are all ways to contribute meaningfully. The key is to act in alignment with one's values and capabilities, knowing that every effort matters.

Critically, individual action is not a substitute for systemic change but a complement to it. Large-scale reforms require collective efforts, but those efforts are often sparked and sustained by individuals who refuse to accept the status quo. By modeling the changes we want to see, we create a ripple effect that influences those around us and lays the groundwork for broader transformations. Individual actions serve as the seeds of change, growing into movements that reshape societies.

As we move forward in this chapter, we will explore practical ways to harness the power of individual action. From cultivating empathy in our personal relationships to advocating for change in our communities, the steps we take as individuals can have a profound impact. The goal is not to solve every problem on our own but to recognize the role we play in the larger mosaic of progress. When we embrace our ability to make a difference, we empower ourselves and others to work toward a future that reflects our highest aspirations.

Ultimately, the question is not whether individual actions matter—they do. The question is whether we are willing to take responsibility for the role we can play in shaping the world around us. By acknowledging our agency and choosing to act with intention, we can contribute to a society where equity, understanding, and progress are not just ideals but realities. This chapter is an invitation to reflect on the power of our choices and to embrace the opportunity to be part of the change we wish to see.

Fostering Empathy and Understanding

Empathy and understanding are powerful tools for bridging divides and fostering meaningful connections in a polarized world. At their core, these qualities allow us to see others as individuals with unique experiences, values, and emotions, rather than as representatives of opposing ideologies or stereotypes. In an era where divisions seem to dominate our social and political landscapes, the ability to genuinely listen and engage with others offers a way to rebuild trust and create a foundation for collective progress.

Active listening is one of the simplest yet most impactful ways to cultivate empathy. Too often, conversations devolve into debates where each party is more focused on formulating a rebuttal than understanding the other's perspective. Active listening flips this dynamic, encouraging us to hear what others are saying without judgment or interruption. This doesn't mean agreeing with everything we hear—it means being present and open to understanding where someone else is coming from. By doing so, we not only validate their experience but also create space for mutual respect and dialogue.

Engaging in respectful dialogue is equally important. In a world dominated by sound bites and online echo chambers, it's easy to retreat into spaces where our own beliefs are constantly reinforced. However, growth and understanding occur when we step outside of these comfort zones. Respectful dialogue involves approaching conversations with curiosity rather than defensiveness, asking questions to clarify rather than to challenge. It's about finding common ground, even in the midst of disagreement, and recognizing that differing perspectives can coexist without diminishing our own.

One actionable way to foster empathy and understanding is by intentionally seeking out opportunities to engage with people from different backgrounds. This could mean attending community events, joining a group or organization that includes a diverse range of members, or simply striking up conversations with neighbors or coworkers who hold different views. These interactions, while seemingly small, have the potential to break down preconceived notions and replace them with genuine human connections. Over time, these relationships can build bridges across divides, making it easier to collaborate on shared goals.

Participating in storytelling initiatives or community dialogues can also be transformative. Hearing firsthand accounts of others' experiences helps to humanize complex issues and challenges us to reconsider our assumptions. For example, someone who has never experienced systemic injustice may gain a deeper understanding by listening to the personal stories of those who have. Similarly, someone who holds strong political views may find common ground with others by focusing on shared values rather than partisan differences. Storytelling has the unique ability to bypass intellectual defenses and connect on an emotional level, fostering empathy in ways that statistics and arguments often cannot.

Empathy is not just a personal virtue—it is a societal necessity. When we approach others with empathy, we create an environment where collaboration and problem-solving become possible. Empathy allows us to navigate complex issues with nuance and compassion, recognizing that most people, even those we disagree with, are motivated by values and beliefs they hold dear. By understanding these motivations, we can address conflicts in a way that seeks solutions rather than perpetuating division.

Cultivating empathy also requires us to confront our own biases and assumptions. It's natural to view the world through the lens of our own experiences, but this can lead to blind spots when it comes to understanding others. Taking the time to reflect on our own perspectives and how they might differ from those of others is a critical step in fostering empathy. This self-awareness not only improves our ability to connect with others but also enhances our own growth and understanding.

The workplace is another area where fostering empathy and understanding can have a profound impact. Diverse teams thrive when members approach each other with openness and respect, valuing the unique perspectives and contributions that each individual brings. Leaders who prioritize empathy create environments where employees feel heard and valued, leading to higher levels of collaboration, innovation, and overall satisfaction. By modeling empathy in professional settings, we can set a standard that extends beyond the workplace and into broader societal interactions.

Ultimately, fostering empathy and understanding is about choosing connection over division. It's about recognizing that every person has a story worth hearing and that our differences, while real, do not have to define us. By engaging with others in a spirit of curiosity and respect, we can begin to dismantle the barriers that keep us apart and work together to create a more inclusive and compassionate society.

As individuals, we have the power to set the tone for the relationships and communities we are part of. When we choose to listen actively, engage respectfully, and prioritize empathy, we create a ripple effect that can influence others to do the same. The tools for fostering understanding are simple but powerful, and they are available to each of us, every day. By embracing these tools, we can take meaningful steps toward building bridges, healing divides, and contributing to a society where connection and collaboration prevail over polarization.

Supporting Local and Grassroods

Supporting local and grassroots efforts is one of the most impactful ways individuals can drive meaningful change in their communities. While systemic issues like housing inequality, education disparities, and healthcare access may feel insurmountable on a national scale, local initiatives provide tangible opportunities to make a difference. These efforts demonstrate that collective action at the community level can create ripples that contribute to broader societal progress.

Volunteering with local organizations is a direct and powerful way to contribute. Whether it's working at a food pantry, tutoring students in underserved schools, or participating in community health initiatives, these actions address immediate needs while building stronger, more connected neighborhoods. For example, community gardens not only provide fresh produce in food deserts but also foster collaboration among neighbors, bridging divides and creating a sense of shared purpose. By dedicating time and resources to these initiatives, individuals can help address pressing issues while building relationships that strengthen the social fabric.

Grassroots movements play a critical role in advocating for systemic change, often starting at the local level before gaining momentum nationally. These movements are fueled by individuals who see a need for change and are willing to mobilize others toward a common goal. For instance, local campaigns to increase affordable housing or improve public transportation often originate with grassroots advocacy. These efforts rely on the participation of ordinary citizens who are passionate about their communities and committed to creating positive change.

One way to support grassroots movements is by attending town hall meetings, joining advocacy groups, or participating in local organizing efforts. These actions not only amplify the voices of marginalized communities but also ensure that decisions are made with input from those most affected. By getting involved in these spaces, individuals can influence policies and initiatives that directly impact their neighborhoods. Grassroots activism thrives on collaboration, and every contribution—whether it's time, expertise, or financial support—adds value to the movement.

Community initiatives also demonstrate the power of individual contributions. Successful examples abound, from neighborhood clean-up drives that transform public spaces to mentorship programs that help young people realize their potential. These initiatives remind us that small actions, when multiplied by many, can lead to significant outcomes. For instance, local efforts to address homelessness, such as building tiny home villages or providing transitional housing, often start with a few dedicated individuals who mobilize their communities to act. These projects not only provide immediate relief but also inspire others to replicate similar models in their areas.

Beyond direct involvement, individuals can support local and grassroots efforts by using their voices and networks to raise awareness. Sharing information about community events, fundraisers, or advocacy campaigns on social media can help expand their reach and attract new supporters. Writing letters to local representatives or speaking at public forums can also amplify the concerns of grassroots movements, ensuring they receive the attention they deserve. Advocacy at this level often lays the groundwork for broader policy changes, highlighting the interconnectedness of local and national efforts.

One of the most powerful aspects of grassroots movements is their ability to empower marginalized communities to lead. When individuals from these communities take ownership of initiatives, they bring lived experiences and unique perspectives that are essential for creating effective and sustainable solutions. Supporting grassroots leaders by offering resources, mentorship, or simply amplifying their voices is a crucial step toward equity and inclusion. It shifts the narrative from "helping" communities to empowering them to advocate for themselves, fostering long-term resilience and self-determination.

Engaging with local efforts also provides an opportunity for personal growth and learning. By working alongside people from diverse backgrounds, individuals can gain a deeper understanding of the challenges others face and the systemic factors that contribute to inequality. This firsthand exposure can be transformative, fostering empathy and a stronger commitment to social justice. It also breaks down stereotypes and misconceptions, replacing them with authentic relationships and shared goals.

Ultimately, supporting local and grassroots efforts is about taking ownership of the change we wish to see. It's about recognizing that each of us has a role to play in building a more equitable and inclusive society, starting in our own backyards. These efforts may not always make headlines, but they create real, lasting impacts for the people and communities involved. By participating in or supporting grassroots movements, individuals become part of a collective force that drives systemic change from the ground up.

Change doesn't always require grand gestures or sweeping reforms; it often begins with small, meaningful actions within our own communities. By volunteering, advocating, and supporting grassroots leaders, we can help address local issues while contributing to larger societal goals. Together, these efforts create a foundation for a more just and equitable future, proving that the power to make a difference lies within each of us.

Advocating for Policy Changes

Advocating for policy changes is one of the most direct and impactful ways individuals can contribute to systemic reform. While personal choices and community involvement lay the groundwork for change, engaging with the political system amplifies those efforts and ensures they reach the decision-makers who can enact lasting reforms. Advocacy transforms individual concerns into collective action, creating momentum for meaningful policy shifts.

One of the simplest yet most effective methods of advocacy is contacting elected officials. Politicians are responsive to public opinion, and emails, letters, or phone calls can influence their priorities. When individuals express support for policies such as equitable school funding, environmental protections, or healthcare reforms, it signals that these issues are important to their constituents. Thoughtful, well-articulated communication helps bridge the gap between citizens and policymakers, fostering accountability and responsiveness.

Signing petitions and supporting advocacy campaigns are additional ways to contribute to larger movements. Petitions demonstrate collective support for an issue, creating a visible demand for change. Advocacy campaigns, often organized by nonprofits or grassroots organizations, provide structured opportunities to contribute, from participating in rallies to amplifying messages on social media. These efforts show that public support for a cause extends beyond individual voices, making it harder for policymakers to ignore.

Voting remains the cornerstone of political advocacy. Elections determine the policymakers who will shape laws and allocate resources, directly influencing issues like education, healthcare, and economic policy. Staying informed about candidates and their platforms is critical for making choices that align with one's values. However, advocacy doesn't end at the ballot box. Supporting voter registration drives, encouraging turnout in underrepresented communities, and staying engaged between election cycles ensure that democratic participation remains robust and inclusive.

Effective advocacy also requires individuals to be informed about the issues they care about. Staying updated on legislative developments, understanding the nuances of proposed policies, and engaging in meaningful conversations with peers are all essential components of impactful advocacy. Knowledge equips individuals to articulate their positions clearly, counter misinformation, and build support for reforms that align with shared goals. Informed advocates can rally others to the cause, creating a ripple effect of engagement and action.

Collective efforts in advocacy have already led to significant achievements, from environmental protections to advancements in civil rights. These successes highlight the power of persistence and unity. Policy changes often take time, and setbacks are inevitable, but sustained engagement can build momentum and ultimately lead to progress. Advocacy is a reminder that change is not immediate but requires commitment and collaboration.

Advocating for policy changes also includes amplifying the voices of marginalized communities. This involves supporting initiatives that address systemic inequities and ensuring that policies are inclusive. Advocacy rooted in empathy and equity

215

creates a more representative society, where everyone has a stake in the benefits of progress.

Ultimately, advocating for policy changes empowers individuals to take control of their futures and contribute to a collective vision of a more equitable society. By leveraging tools such as contacting representatives, participating in advocacy campaigns, and voting, individuals can transform their values into action. Advocacy reminds us that systemic change is possible when individuals come together to push for reforms that reflect shared aspirations for justice, opportunity, and equality.

Practicing Sustainable Personal Growth

Practicing sustainable personal growth is a cornerstone of contributing to societal progress. While systemic change often requires collective action, the foundation of such movements begins with individuals who commit to aligning their personal values with their daily habits and decisions. Growth, in this sense, is not about perfection but about consistency—a willingness to learn, adapt, and take responsibility for one's impact on the world.

One of the most effective ways to sustain personal growth is through self-education. Learning about issues such as inequality, polarization, and cultural understanding empowers individuals to make informed decisions and engage in meaningful conversations. Books, podcasts, workshops, and documentaries provide accessible avenues for gaining knowledge, broadening perspectives, and challenging assumptions. For instance, reading about the history of systemic inequities or listening to firsthand accounts from marginalized communities fosters empathy and a deeper understanding of the challenges society must address.

Personal accountability is another essential component of sustainable growth. This means reflecting on one's actions and ensuring they align with stated values. For example, if equity and inclusion are core principles, individuals can evaluate how their choices—such as where they shop, the media they consume, or the organizations they support—reflect those ideals. Personal accountability is not about self-criticism but about recognizing areas for improvement and committing to continuous progress. Consistency in these efforts, even in small ways, builds a foundation for meaningful impact over time.

Adopting small, intentional lifestyle changes can also make a significant difference. Supporting ethical businesses, reducing waste, or mentoring someone from an underrepresented background are actions that create tangible benefits for others while reinforcing personal values. These habits may seem minor in isolation, but their cumulative effect can ripple outward, inspiring others and contributing to broader societal progress. When individuals make deliberate choices to uplift others or reduce harm, they embody the principles of equity and sustainability in their daily lives.

Sustainable personal growth also requires resilience. Change is rarely linear, and setbacks are inevitable. Whether it's encountering resistance when advocating for a cause or grappling with personal biases, growth demands patience and persistence. Maintaining a growth mindset—one that views challenges as opportunities for learning rather than failures—enables individuals to remain committed to their goals. This perspective fosters long-term progress, ensuring that efforts to create positive change are not fleeting but enduring.

As this chapter concludes, it is vital to emphasize the interconnectedness of personal growth and societal transformation. Every action, no matter how small, contributes to the larger movement toward unity and equity. By fostering empathy, supporting local initiatives, advocating for change, and practicing sustainable growth, individuals play an integral role in shaping a brighter future. Growth is not a solitary journey; it is a shared commitment to building a world that reflects the values of justice, opportunity, and inclusion.

In the next chapter, we will explore how these individual efforts can coalesce into collective action, creating systemic solutions to the challenges we face. Together, we will examine how the power of community amplifies individual contributions, turning aspirations into realities and paving the way for lasting progress. The path ahead may not be easy, but it is one worth pursuing—for ourselves and for the generations to come.

A Unified Tomorrow

Imagine waking up in a world where the biggest challenges of humanity have been overcome, not through isolated efforts, but through collective determination and cooperation. The air is clean, the streets buzz with life, and technology seamlessly integrates into everyday routines to make life easier and more enjoyable. This is a world where cancer is no longer a feared diagnosis but a historical footnote—a testament to what humanity can achieve when diverse minds come together to tackle the seemingly impossible. It is a world where the climate is stable, ecosystems thrive, and every child can grow up knowing that their potential is not bound by the circumstances of their birth.

This future was not inevitable. It was built on the foundation of shared goals and inclusivity. By valuing the contributions of every individual, regardless of their background, humanity unlocked a wellspring of innovation, compassion, and creativity. Communities that once stood divided found strength in collaboration, proving that progress accelerates when no one is left behind. This transformation wasn't just about solving problems; it was about creating a society where joy, fulfillment, and purpose are accessible to everyone.

The breakthroughs of this new era are extraordinary. Diseases that once seemed insurmountable, like Alzheimer's, heart disease, and cancer, have been eradicated through advances in personalized medicine and global research partnerships. Renewable energy powers homes and businesses, with solar panels and wind turbines blending seamlessly into urban and rural landscapes. Food is plentiful, sustainably produced, and available to all, eliminating hunger as a pressing concern. Technology has been harnessed for the collective good, from AI tools that streamline work to transportation systems that are efficient, eco-friendly, and accessible to everyone.

The most remarkable change, however, is not just in the innovations but in the way people live. Diverse communities thrive as people from all walks of life come together to celebrate their differences and build on their shared dreams. Festivals of culture, music, and art are commonplace, drawing crowds eager to learn and connect. Schools emphasize creativity, collaboration, and emotional intelligence, preparing children not just to succeed but to contribute meaningfully to society. Public spaces are vibrant hubs of activity, where laughter, conversation, and shared purpose define daily life.

This world was made possible by one unshakable truth: unity is humanity's greatest strength. By focusing on what connects rather than divides, people have created a society that values inclusivity, equity, and empathy. This chapter is a glimpse into what can happen when we choose to work together, prioritizing shared goals over individual gain. It's a vision of a future that is not only possible but within reach—a future that invites each of us to imagine, to hope, and to act.

The fight against cancer and other chronic illnesses was once a long, arduous battle, consuming resources, hope, and lives. But in this unified future, the story of humanity's triumph over disease stands as a shining example of what we can achieve when we work together. Cancer, a word that once struck fear into the hearts of millions, has been eradicated. This breakthrough wasn't the product of isolated labs or narrow-minded thinking—it was the culmination of a global effort that pooled knowledge, perspectives, and ingenuity from every corner of the world.

Diverse teams of researchers, engineers, and clinicians brought their unique insights to the table. Scientists in India and Brazil pioneered cost-effective diagnostic tools, while geneticists in Kenya and Japan refined personalized treatment protocols. Together, they discovered new pathways to eliminate cancer cells without harming healthy tissue, leading to therapies that are affordable and universally accessible. Collaboration replaced competition, allowing solutions to be shared openly and progress to accelerate exponentially.

The advancements didn't stop there. Regenerative medicine revolutionized the way we approach health. Using stem cells and bioengineered tissues, damaged organs can now be repaired or even replaced entirely. Patients no longer endure years on waiting lists for transplants; instead, personalized organs are grown in labs, tailored to their unique genetic makeup. These developments have not only extended lifespans but also enhanced the quality of life for millions, allowing individuals to live without the burden of chronic illness or disability.

Personalized healthcare has also flourished, transforming medicine from reactive to preventive. Comprehensive genome mapping, once a luxury for the wealthy, is now a standard procedure at birth. This allows healthcare providers to identify potential health risks before they manifest, empowering individuals to make lifestyle adjustments or receive targeted treatments to prevent diseases entirely. Imagine a world where heart attacks are as rare as smallpox, and diabetes is managed so effectively that it no longer shortens lives. This is the reality that inclusivity and innovation have created.

The ripple effects of these medical breakthroughs are profound. Families no longer face the financial and emotional devastation of losing loved ones to preventable diseases. Parents watch their children grow up without the shadow of hereditary illnesses looming over them. Elderly individuals remain active and engaged in their communities, contributing wisdom and experience to younger generations. These medical miracles have brought unparalleled joy and relief, allowing people to live longer, fuller lives.

In this new era, healthcare is not a privilege but a universal right. Clinics and hospitals are accessible to all, regardless of income or location. Advances in telemedicine mean that even the most remote communities can receive world-class care, bridging the gap between urban and rural areas. The fear of unaffordable medical bills is a thing of the past, replaced by a system that values well-being over profit.

Perhaps the most inspiring aspect of this medical revolution is the renewed sense of humanity it has cultivated. People of all backgrounds—rich and poor, young and old, urban and rural— now share a profound appreciation for life and the interconnectedness of health. The collaborative effort to cure diseases has not only transformed medicine but also strengthened the bonds between individuals and nations. It reminds us that when we prioritize collective well-being, we unlock possibilities that benefit everyone.

In this world, joy replaces sorrow, and relief follows despair. Children thrive, parents rejoice, and elders cherish their golden years, knowing they are surrounded by the love and support of a healthier, happier society. The eradication of cancer and other chronic illnesses is more than a scientific triumph; it is a testament to the power of unity and the boundless potential of the human spirit. This chapter of our shared story reminds us that when we stand together, there is no challenge too great, no dream too bold, and no future out of reach.

In this transformed future, the planet has been reclaimed, rejuvenated, and reimagined. Once on the brink of ecological collapse, Earth now thrives as a testament to humanity's collective will to change. Through global cooperation and groundbreaking innovations in climate control and environmental technology, the air is cleaner, the oceans teem with life, and ecosystems once thought lost have been restored.

At the heart of this revolution are innovations that reverse pollution and stabilize the planet's delicate ecosystems. Carbon capture technology, perfected through international collaboration, has not only halted the rise of atmospheric CO_2 but actively removes it. Giant machines in desert regions and aboard floating ocean platforms extract carbon from the air, turning it into sustainable building materials or safely storing it deep underground. The result is a dramatic reversal of global warming trends, cooling the planet to pre-industrial levels and mitigating the devastating effects of climate change.

Renewable energy is no longer a luxury or niche solution; it is the backbone of human civilization. Solar panels with near-perfect efficiency line rooftops, highways, and deserts, while advanced wind turbines harness even the gentlest breezes. In coastal cities, tidal power stations generate clean energy from the rhythm of the seas. Rural areas thrive with localized energy systems, ensuring that every home, farm, and business has access to reliable, sustainable power. Energy is abundant and inexpensive, fueling economies while reducing the strain on natural resources.

Green cities have emerged as shining examples of this new world. Urban centers once choked by smog now boast lush vertical gardens and tree-lined streets that cool the air and provide fresh produce for local communities. Public transportation is powered by renewable energy, making cars a rare sight in bustling metropolises. Smart infrastructure ensures waste is minimized, with water and materials recycled seamlessly through advanced systems. Parks and green spaces dominate cityscapes, inviting residents to gather, exercise, and connect with nature. In these cities, the concept of "urban living" has been redefined, blending the convenience of modern technology with the serenity of the natural world.

Rural areas, too, have reaped the benefits of this green revolution. Precision agriculture, powered by AI and renewable energy, allows farmers to maximize yields while conserving water and soil health. Biodiversity corridors stretch across continents, enabling wildlife to flourish alongside human activity. Remote communities, once left behind in the energy transition, are now powered by solar and wind farms, enjoying the same access to clean resources as their urban counterparts. These advancements have fostered economic opportunities, transforming rural regions into vibrant, self-sustaining hubs.

Global cooperation has been instrumental in achieving these outcomes. Nations set aside rivalries to tackle climate change as a shared challenge, forming coalitions that pool resources, expertise, and technology. Annual environmental summits bring together scientists, policymakers, and activists from every corner of the globe to celebrate achievements and address remaining challenges. Through these collaborations, humanity has preserved the Amazon rainforest, restored coral reefs, and reforested vast swaths of land, creating a greener, more livable world for all.

Preserving natural resources is no longer seen as a sacrifice but as an investment in the future. Education campaigns instill a deep respect for the environment in every generation, fostering a culture of stewardship and sustainability. Young people grow up learning how their choices—whether in consumption, energy use, or career paths—impact the planet. This collective awareness has led to a dramatic shift in societal values, where economic growth and environmental preservation are no longer in conflict but mutually reinforcing.

The most profound impact of this greener world is on the quality of life it provides. Clean air and water are universal rights, not privileges. Heatwaves and extreme weather events, once deadly and destructive, have become rare occurrences thanks to advanced climate modeling and mitigation technologies. Families enjoy outdoor activities without fear of pollution or environmental hazards. Children grow up exploring forests, rivers, and oceans that are vibrant and full of life, fostering a deep connection to the natural world.

This new era is not without its challenges, but the shared commitment to addressing them has created a global sense of purpose and unity. Humanity has learned that the key to solving complex problems lies in cooperation, innovation, and the willingness to act. In this world, the air is cleaner, the future is brighter, and the planet itself is a testament to what we can achieve when we prioritize the well-being of both people and the

Earth.

The story of climate control and environmental restoration is a story of hope, perseverance, and the power of collective action. It reminds us that even in the face of the direst circumstances, humanity has the capacity to adapt, innovate, and overcome. By embracing the principles of sustainability and inclusivity, we have not only saved our planet but also created a world where life—for every being—is worth living.

The global economy thrives on the principles of inclusivity, innovation, and sustainability. Companies, driven by a commitment to ethical practices and diverse leadership, have unlocked unprecedented growth and prosperity. This is a world where businesses flourish not by exploiting resources and people but by empowering workers, embracing technological advancements, and prioritizing long-term well-being. The result is a robust economy where goods and services are affordable, workers are valued, and prosperity is shared.

At the heart of this economic abundance is the belief that inclusivity drives innovation. Companies have recognized that diverse teams bring varied perspectives, enabling them to solve problems creatively and develop products that resonate with a global audience. Businesses no longer see diversity as a mere checkbox but as a strategic advantage. Leadership positions are filled by individuals from all walks of life, creating decision-making processes that reflect the values and needs of a broad consumer base. This shift has fostered a corporate culture of collaboration and mutual respect, leading to groundbreaking innovations in every sector.

Affordable goods and services are a hallmark of this new economy. Advances in technology, particularly automation and artificial intelligence, have drastically reduced production costs without compromising quality or worker welfare. Factories operate efficiently with minimal waste, producing everything from food to electronics at a fraction of the cost seen in the past. Supply chains have been reimagined for both speed and sustainability, ensuring that essential goods are accessible to everyone, regardless of location or income.

For consumers, this has translated into an era of affordability. Basic necessities like food, clothing, and housing are no longer sources of financial strain. The cost of living has decreased significantly, allowing families to focus on building wealth, pursuing education, or enjoying leisure activities. Luxuries that were once reserved for the wealthy, such as advanced medical treatments or international travel, have become accessible to the middle and working classes. This democratization of goods and services has fostered a sense of shared prosperity, reducing economic inequalities and increasing social cohesion.

Workers, once seen as expendable resources in many industries, are now at the center of corporate success. Companies have embraced fair wages, comprehensive benefits, and flexible working conditions as standard practices. Universal childcare, extended parental leave, and mental health support are no longer perks but rights enjoyed by all employees. This commitment to worker well-being has resulted in a motivated and loyal workforce, driving productivity and innovation to new heights.

The rise of cooperative business models has also contributed to this economic abundance. Employee-owned enterprises and profit-sharing initiatives have given workers a direct stake in their companies' success. This has not only increased job satisfaction but also fostered a sense of shared responsibility for organizational outcomes. Communities have benefited as well, as locally owned businesses reinvest profits into neighborhood improvements, creating a virtuous cycle of growth and prosperity.

Technological advancements have played a crucial role in shaping this world of abundance. Smart automation has revolutionized industries, from agriculture to manufacturing, enabling higher yields and faster production times. Renewable energy technologies, such as solar panels and wind turbines, have become affordable and widely adopted, significantly reducing energy costs for households and businesses. Artificial intelligence assists in everything from logistics to healthcare, streamlining processes and improving outcomes.

In this new economy, the benefits of technological progress are distributed equitably. Governments and private organizations have collaborated to ensure that no one is left behind in the technological revolution. Public programs provide free or low-cost access to digital tools and training, enabling individuals to adapt to changing job markets and take advantage of new opportunities. Education systems have integrated STEM and digital literacy into their core curricula, preparing the next generation to thrive in a tech-driven world.

Global cooperation has been a key driver of this economic transformation. Nations have come together to establish fair trade agreements, promote cross-border collaboration, and support developing economies. These efforts have created a more interconnected world, where resources and knowledge flow freely, benefiting everyone. The era of cutthroat competition has given way to one of collective advancement, where countries work together to address challenges and seize opportunities.

Small businesses and entrepreneurs have flourished in this environment, supported by microloans, mentorship programs, and accessible marketplaces. Innovations that start in garages or small workshops now have a clear path to global impact, thanks to platforms that connect creators with consumers worldwide. This has democratized entrepreneurship, allowing individuals from diverse backgrounds to turn their ideas into thriving businesses.

Perhaps the most significant outcome of this economic abundance is its impact on quality of life. With financial pressures alleviated, people have more time and resources to pursue their passions, nurture relationships, and contribute to their communities. Art, culture, and scientific research have entered a golden age, fueled by the creativity and collaboration of individuals unburdened by economic hardship.

The health of the planet has also benefited from this shift in priorities. Sustainable business practices, once seen as costly and optional, are now integral to economic success. Companies compete to develop the most eco-friendly products and processes, knowing that consumers demand accountability and innovation in equal measure. Circular economies, where waste is minimized, and resources are reused, have become the norm, ensuring that economic growth does not come at the expense of environmental health.

As the world moves forward, this economic transformation serves as a reminder of what is possible when inclusivity, innovation, and sustainability are prioritized. It shows that prosperity is not a finite resource but a shared opportunity, capable of lifting everyone when harnessed responsibly. In this future, companies flourish, goods are affordable, and life is not just livable but profoundly fulfilling.

This vision of economic abundance challenges us to rethink what success means. It is not measured solely by GDP or corporate profits but by the well-being of individuals, the health of communities, and the sustainability of our planet. It is a future built on shared goals and collective effort, where everyone has a role to play and everyone stands to benefit. By investing in people, fostering innovation, and embracing the principles of equity and sustainability, we can create a world where economic abundance is not a dream but a reality for all.

In a world transformed by unity and innovation, living longer is no longer a dream but a shared reality, made meaningful by an enhanced quality of life. Advancements in health, science, and technology have extended human lifespans, allowing people to experience more of life's joys while contributing to society in new and enriching ways. The focus is no longer just on adding years to life but on making those years vibrant, fulfilling, and deeply connected to personal and collective purpose.

In this era, multi-generational families thrive together in communities designed to celebrate and support every stage of life. Elders, once marginalized in many societies, are recognized for their wisdom and experience, contributing actively to community decisions, mentorship programs, and even new career paths. Children grow up surrounded by the love and guidance of grandparents, who play an active role in their lives, creating a powerful sense of belonging and continuity. Societies are structured to ensure that people of all ages feel valued, from policies promoting intergenerational housing to inclusive workspaces that adapt to the needs of older and younger individuals alike.

With longer lifespans comes the opportunity to embrace life's diversity in ways previously unimaginable. Careers are no longer linear journeys with a single destination; instead, individuals explore multiple fields over their lifetimes. A person might spend two decades as a scientist, another as an artist, and yet another as an entrepreneur or teacher. Education systems are designed to support this lifelong learning, offering flexible, accessible opportunities for skill-building and personal growth at every age. People no longer feel the pressure to "have it all" by 30 or 40—they have the gift of time to discover themselves and evolve.

The breakthroughs that extend life go beyond medical cures to include wellness technologies that enhance daily living. Smart devices monitor health in real time, providing early detection of potential issues and tailored recommendations for diet, exercise, and stress management. Innovations in mental health care ensure that longevity is accompanied by emotional well-being, with therapies and support systems readily available to maintain balance and resilience. Workplaces and communities alike prioritize wellness, incorporating green spaces, meditation centers, and health-focused initiatives to ensure people thrive holistically.

In this future, aging is not seen as a decline but as a dynamic phase filled with potential. People in their 80s and 90s are active participants in society, traveling, inventing, or mentoring younger generations. Technologies like regenerative medicine and bioengineering have minimized the physical limitations of aging, enabling people to remain energetic and engaged. Retirement as it once existed has evolved into a flexible concept—individuals transition between working, learning, and leisure throughout their lives, finding fulfillment in balance.

The extended lifespan has also fostered deeper connections

among individuals and communities. With more time to spend with loved ones and a stronger sense of intergenerational responsibility, people are more invested in creating a better world for the future. Long life expectancy has brought about a shared appreciation for sustainability, peace, and collaboration, as the consequences of today's actions are now felt directly by those who make them.

This is a world where living longer is not about defying mortality but about embracing life more fully. The time gained is spent nurturing relationships, exploring passions, and making meaningful contributions to society. By fostering inclusion, innovation, and sustainability, humanity has created a future where longevity is a shared gift, not a privilege of the few. It's a future where people don't just live longer—they live better.

Americans have a choice: to lead the way in building this better future or to watch as another nation steps into the role of global pioneer. The United States has a unique opportunity to redefine leadership, not through dominance or conflict but by setting an example of innovation, equity, and inclusivity. This is a call to action—not just for policymakers and leaders, but for every citizen—to embrace the values that can make this vision a reality.

The future belongs to those who dare to imagine it and work to make it happen. By uniting around shared goals and fostering a society of empathy and collaboration, Americans can realize the dreams that have long defined their identity. This is not just a dream for a better America; it is a call for a better world, with the United States as a beacon of what is possible when unity triumphs over division. Let us choose to lead—not with hatred or fear, but with hope, courage, and a commitment to a brighter tomorrow.

The dazzling future we've envisioned—where diseases are cured, the climate is stabilized, prosperity is abundant, and lives are long and fulfilling—rests on a foundation of equality and inclusivity. This is the catch: achieving such a world requires a collective commitment to shared goals and a willingness to embrace diversity as a strength. It is not enough to dream; we must act, together, with the understanding that our differences enrich us and that progress for one group uplifts us all.

The breakthroughs that transformed this imagined world—from medical miracles to economic abundance—were not achieved by chance but through deliberate collaboration. By prioritizing shared goals over individual or partisan interests, humanity unlocked opportunities that had previously seemed unattainable. Equality and inclusivity were not afterthoughts; they were the catalysts that made innovation possible and prosperity sustainable.

When we build a society that values every person, we tap into the full potential of human creativity, resilience, and ambition. We create a world where barriers to progress are dismantled, where opportunity is not hoarded but shared, and where joy and fulfillment are not privileges for the few but the reality for the many. This is the promise of unity: a future where the success of one is the success of all.

The path forward is not without its challenges. The divisions and inequities we face today can feel insurmountable, but history has shown us that change begins with small, intentional actions. Every conversation that fosters understanding, every policy that prioritizes equity, and every effort to lift up others contributes to the broader movement toward a better world. This book has explored the systemic changes and individual actions needed to bridge divides, and now it's up to us to carry those lessons forward.

We must remember that equality is not a zero-sum game. Happiness is not diminished by being shared—it multiplies. Progress is not achieved by leaving others behind; it is accelerated when everyone is given the chance to thrive.

As we close, envision the role you play in this story. The future is not something that happens to us; it is something we create together. Every action you take—no matter how small—can be a step toward the inclusive, prosperous, and united world we aspire to build. Together, through equality, empathy, and shared purpose, we can steer it toward a horizon of hope, happiness, and progress. The choice is ours—let us make it wisely.

Crafting a Book with 125 Sources: The Journey Behind the Pages

When I first set out to write this book, I had no idea it would lead me down a rabbit hole of over 125 sources, each offering a piece of a much larger puzzle. What started as an ambitious project quickly turned into an exhaustive journey through data, opinions, studies, and stories. This process not only shaped the book you're holding but also taught me lessons about the complexity of truth, the importance of diversity in perspectives, and the delicate balance between optimism and realism.

Why 125 sources? To some, that number might seem excessive for a single book, but to me, it was a necessity. Writing about issues as complex as inequality, polarization, climate change, and the potential of humanity demands more than one perspective or one type of expertise. Every source served as a thread in a much larger tapestry, helping me weave together a story that is as comprehensive and informed as possible.

For instance, I didn't just pull statistics from one government report and call it a day. I compared data from think tanks, academic studies, journalistic investigations, and grassroots organizations. Each source added another dimension to my understanding, forcing me to consider multiple angles. When writing about economic inequality, I dove into the numbers from institutions like the World Bank and the U.S. Census Bureau, but I also read personal stories from people living paycheck to paycheck. These contrasting perspectives gave me a clearer picture of both the macro-level trends and the micro-level human impact.

The depth of research also led to an unexpected consequence: I needed a separate special edition just to give my sources the space they deserve. This isn't just a book filled with endnotes and a dry bibliography—it's an invitation to dig deeper. I included the special edition because I believe in the power of information and transparency. If something in this book resonates with you or makes you question your beliefs, you can trace it back to its source and explore further.

This process isn't about me proving I did my homework; it's about empowering you as the reader to engage critically with the material. Every fact, every quote, and every statistic came from somewhere, and I want you to have access to those origins. Whether you're a student, a policymaker, or just someone curious about the world, I hope the special edition helps you see how this book was built—and inspires you to start your own exploration.

Using 125 sources wasn't just about gathering a lot of information—it was about gathering the right kind of information. Diversity in sourcing was a priority from the beginning. I didn't want this book to lean too heavily on one ideology, one region, or one type of expertise. To paint a full picture, I needed to include voices from different sectors, cultures, and lived experiences.

Take climate change, for example. I pulled from scientific journals to understand the data, grassroots organizations to see how communities are fighting back, and economic analyses to grasp the financial stakes. But I also included perspectives from Indigenous activists, whose ancestral knowledge offers invaluable insights into environmental stewardship. By weaving these threads together, I aimed to create a narrative that respects complexity and avoids the trap of oversimplification.

The same approach applied to other topics, like education and economic inequality. I included conservative voices arguing for market-driven solutions and progressive thinkers advocating for systemic reforms. This balance was essential for crafting a book that doesn't just preach to the choir but challenges all readers to think critically about the issues at hand.

As proud as I am of the book's scope and depth, I'll admit something: I fell into the trap of being too optimistic. When you're surrounded by groundbreaking research, inspiring success stories, and glimpses of what humanity could achieve, it's easy to lean into an idealized vision of the future. I wanted this book to motivate people, to make them believe in the possibility of change. But in doing so, I risked making the challenges seem smaller than they are—or the solutions easier to implement than reality allows.

For instance, when I wrote about curing cancer through global collaboration or tackling climate change with innovative technology, I painted a picture that felt within reach. But the truth is, these breakthroughs require more than just effort; they demand structural changes, sustained funding, and a willingness to confront uncomfortable truths. They also require patience—a quality often in short supply in a world hungry for quick fixes.

The optimistic tone wasn't unintentional, but I now see how it might come across as overly simplistic in some parts. The reality is, progress is messy. It's slow, full of setbacks, and often met with resistance. By leaning too heavily on what could be, I may have underplayed the hard work it takes to get there.

Another thing I've noticed is the book's amcedic tone—a term I use to describe its almost anthem-like quality. In trying to inspire and uplift, I sometimes veered into a tone that might feel overly grand or idealistic. While some readers might find this energizing, others may feel it glosses over the grit and struggle inherent in systemic change.

I wanted this book to be a rallying cry, but I recognize that it might also need to be a reckoning. Acknowledging the messiness, the failures, and the compromises doesn't make the vision less powerful—it makes it more real. As I reflect on this, I hope future editions or readers' interpretations will balance the anthem with the reality.

At the end of the day, this book is an invitation—a starting point, not an endpoint. I don't have all the answers, and I don't expect anyone to agree with every conclusion I've drawn. What I hope, though, is that it sparks something in you: curiosity, frustration, hope, or even a desire to challenge what I've written.

I want readers to see this as a blueprint, not a prescription. Take what resonates with you, dig into the sources, and form your own opinions. Share them, argue them, refine them. Change doesn't come from one book or one person; it comes from collective effort, from the collision of ideas, and from the willingness to dream of a better world.

Writing this book has been one of the most challenging and rewarding experiences of my life. It's forced me to confront my own biases, question my assumptions, and dive into issues that don't have easy answers. It's also reminded me of the power of stories, the importance of facts, and the potential of people when they work together.

As you close this chapter—whether it's in the standard edition or the special edition with all its sources—I hope you feel a little more equipped to face the challenges ahead. I hope you see the world not just as it is, but as it could be. And most importantly, I hope you see your role in shaping it.

Because the future isn't written yet. It's being written by all of us, one action, one choice, and one conversation at a time. Let's make it a story worth telling.

ACKNOWLEDGMENTS

Writing this book has been one of the most transformative experiences of my life, and I am deeply grateful to the people who supported me, inspired me, and challenged me along the way. This work would not exist without the collective energy of those who encouraged me to think deeply, ask hard questions, and believe in the possibility of a better world.

First and foremost, I want to thank Nicholas for our engaging conversations on the bigger questions in life. You have a remarkable ability to challenge perspectives while remaining open to new ideas, and our discussions pushed me to think more expansively. Whether we were debating the ethics of technological integration or imagining a world free of suffering, your insights left a profound imprint on this book.

To my family, your love and unwavering belief in me have been my foundation. You reminded me, in both subtle and direct ways, of why this work matters—not just to me but to the world we all share. Thank you for your patience as I buried myself in research, writing, and revising, often at the expense of time together.

I am also profoundly grateful to my friends who served as sounding boards for my ideas. Thank you for listening, questioning, and encouraging me to keep going when the weight of this project felt overwhelming. Your feedback gave this book its heart, and your kindness gave me the strength to finish it. To the countless teachers, mentors, and thinkers who shaped my intellectual journey: This book is a reflection of the lessons I've learned from you. You planted the seeds of curiosity and ambition that made this endeavor possible. While I cannot name everyone here, your influence is woven into every page of this work.

I owe a special thanks to the many authors and researchers whose work I drew upon. Your dedication to uncovering truths, no matter how uncomfortable or complex, laid the groundwork for my own exploration. I hope this book adds to the conversations you started and honors the rigor and passion you brought to your fields.

To the readers, thank you for choosing to spend your time with this book. You are the reason I wrote it. My hope is that these pages challenge you, inspire you, and maybe even push you to see the world—and your role in it—a little differently.

Finally, to the people who dream of a better world and work every day to build it: This book is dedicated to you. Your courage, resilience, and vision remind us all that change is possible. It's my deepest hope that this book serves as a companion on your journey, a small piece of the much larger movement we all need to create.

Thank you, truly, for being part of this story.

.

ABOUT THE AUTHOR

Demetri Long is a Harvard College student, entrepreneur, and storyteller with a vision to revolutionize the publishing world. As the Founder and CEO of The Inkwell Publishing Company, he is redefining what it means to publish in the modern era. By focusing on thought-driven innovation, Demetri is creating an ecosystem where authors and readers connect through meaningful, transformative experiences. Demetri believes that publishing is more than an industry-it's a platform for ideas to flourish and inspire. His mission is to foster a community that values creativity, collaboration, and the limitless power of stories to shape the future. Through The Inkwell Publishing Company, he is building a legacy of literature that transcends boundaries and challenges the status quo.

ABOUT THE PUBLISHER

The Inkwell Publishing Company is a forward-thinking literary hub dedicated to reshaping the publishing landscape. The company is driven by the belief that ideas have the power to inspire change, spark creativity, and connect humanity. At The Inkwell, authors are empowered to share their unique voices, and readers are invited into a community that values thought-provoking stories and meaningful engagement.

More than just a publisher, The Inkwell Publishing Company is a platform for innovation and collaboration. It champions new ways of thinking about literature and publishing, challenging traditional norms to create an inclusive, transformative space for creators and audiences alike. Through its commitment to quality, originality, and authenticity, The Inkwell is shaping the future of storytelling—one idea at a time.

www.ingramcontent.com/pod-product-compliance
Lightning Source LLC
Chambersburg PA
CBHW031456120626
46545CB00005B/1624